80!

MEMORIES & REFLECTIONS ON URSULA K. LE GUIN

EDITED BY KAREN JOY FOWLER & DEBBIE NOTKIN

AQUEDUCT PRESS · 2010

Aqueduct Press
PO Box 95787
Seattle WA 99145-2787
www.aqueductpress.com

80! Memories and Reflections on Ursula K. Le Guin

Design & typography by John D. Berry
Cover design by John D. Berry

The text typeface is Adobe Jenson Pro

PHOTOGRAPHS:
Cover photos courtesy of Ursula and Charles Le Guin
Central cover portrait photo by Eileen Gunn.
Frontispiece photo by Brian Attebery.

ISBN: 978-1-933500-43-0
Library of Congress Control Number: 2010931439
First Edition: 2010

9 8 7 6 5 4 3 2 1

CONTENTS

80!

MEMORIES & REFLECTIONS ON
URSULA K. LE GUIN

Rooms Must Explain Themselves

RICHARD CHWEDYK

for Ursula K. Le Guin

THE ROOM has changed so many times
but it is always the same room.
As long as 'always' has been (who knows?),
It is the only 'always' we've got.
It was once a secret attic
and once an empty foyer,
and another time a kitchen
with windows painted shut.
A townhouse living room
radiant in the morning sun.
A bedroom with a bay window
and a ghost.
These rooms are *this* room.
These rooms are inevitable.
These rooms remind me of you.
I don't know if it's because
every forgotten room is a story
or if every story is a forgotten room —
— or that every forgotten room

is a room to be remembered,
but they all remind me of you.
And in every one (though they're all one room)
I find a thrill, both solemn and mischievous,
like the first time my toes
felt the touch of the sea on the beach —
— it's the sea, but gentle, creeping
up the sand, but it's still the sea,
the *whole* sea touching my toes.
It is a room incomprehensible
to all but itself, and instantly familiar.
It is like you.
And it makes me want to pose
a question that you, perhaps,
cannot answer, except in the way
these rooms can answer —
— is it more courageous
to make a dream into something real
or to turn something real into a dream?
It is not the only question
as it is not the only room,
but it is always the question
and always the room
for all the 'always' we've got.

CHICAGO AND MONTREAL, AUGUST 2009

Destinations and Journeys

DEBBIE NOTKIN

IN THE EARLY 1980S, a time I can only revisit through the distorting lens of memory, I fell in love with the women of "Sur," the Latina women who mounted an expedition to Antarctica in 1909, made their way to the South Pole, and decided not to mark it in any way, because "some man longing to be first might come some day, and find it, and know what a fool he had been, and break his heart."

Those women are part of my history. I met them in my 30s and they shaped my ideas of travel and journey and goal and outcome. (They also shaped my ideas of men and women, but those ideas have changed more in the intervening quarter-century than the first set.)

This month, I've been steeped in thinking about Ursula K. Le Guin, the woman and her writing. As I've helped pull together this celebration, the women of "Sur" have been much on my mind.

Le Guin has won many honors, sold many books, and as is so clear from this project has had intense, life-changing, powerful effects on many, many people. And yet, from what I know of her, she evokes in me the women she distilled so powerfully in "Sur": her life, her work, her Ursula-ness seem to be about the journey and not the place-marker. She leads us through strange and familiar landscapes, and encourages us to take what is of value to us, and to leave behind what is there for others to find.

Perhaps, as the poet says, it is better to travel hopefully than to arrive. What I've learned from the women of "Sur" is that the journey is always happening and it is better (for me, at least; for Ursula, perhaps) to choose a direction and pay attention to the terrain than to define the goal.

Thank you, Ursula.

"The Author" and the author and the aspirant

EILEEN GUNN

IN 1975, I decided I would get serious about writing science fiction. I quit my job, dumped all my belongings in my car, and drove across the U.S. to Los Angeles, a city I'd never been to before and in which I knew only one person. My goal was to avoid distraction.

Undistracted, I quickly realized I had no idea what I was doing. It had been a decade since I had regularly read the science-fiction magazines, and although I still read SF avidly, I really had no idea what was current, where the edge was. In mainstream fiction, the edge, for me, was just the other side of Donald Barthelme. I didn't aspire to imitate Barthelme, but I was not interested in writing completely linear fiction. I wanted to pack a bit more into it. What could I get away with?

To find out, I bought copies of Terry Carr's *Best Science Fiction of the Year*, of which there were at that time four volumes. The most recent, #4, contained nine stories by men and one story by a woman. I read all the stories — I don't remember in what order. Of those by men, I have no memory. The story by a woman was "The Author of the Acacia Seeds, and Other Extracts from the *Journal of the Association of Therolinguistics*," by Ursula K. Le Guin.

The story is composed of three articles from a (future) professional journal of a field called, in the story, therolinguistics: the scientific study of the languages of animals. The first extract examines a poem — perhaps a cry of existential despair, perhaps a call to revolution — written in Ant, scrawled in touch-gland exudation on acacia seeds. In the second extract, a researcher rhapsodizes about the kinetic dialects of Penguin and announces an expedition to Antarctica for further study of the emperor penguin's thermal poetry. The third extract is an editorial that urges researchers to look beyond the now-accessible languages of animals to the unknown art of plants, and perhaps even to the slow, opaque poetry of rocks.

In less than 2600 words, the story addresses all of human aspiration — artistic, scientific, philosophic, and emotional communication — and reveals it as only the first step in understanding the universe. It draws, in miniature, a portrait of the history of science and the psychology of scientists: patiently, in painstaking increments, they build structures of knowledge, and ascend those structures to assess their own ignorance and see opportunities for new research. And it sketches three individual researchers, detailing the differences in their personalities: the Ant linguist's clinically precise yet carefully hedged interpretations of text, the Penguin researcher's joyous enthusiasm for spending six months on the ice in the dark to further knowledge of the field, and the journal editor's visionary exhortations to therolinguists everywhere.

The scientists are not the only characters in the story. Within each article is, quickly limned, a tale of non-human emotional lives. The first is a murder mystery with political overtones. The body of a savagely murdered worker ant lay near the poem. Was this the poet? Who killed her? Does the poem call for the overthrow of the queen, or, as a previous researcher suggested, merely express the desire to be an impregnating male? Women have sometimes been killed if perceived to have either aspiration. The second excerpt, in addition to giving a lightning overview of the past (including shout-outs to Konrad Lorenz and John C. Lilly) and intimations, from a 1974 perspective, of the future study of animal language, conveys the varying emotional lives of different types of penguins, and notes that although it was at first thought that they spoke some incomprehensible language related to Dolphin, is was discovered that they in fact speak a perfectly comprehensible avian tongue, because penguins are, after all, birds, not mammals. The third excerpt sets up and amends Tolstoy's definition of Art as communication; it imagines and evokes the "uncommunicative" languages of plants and rocks. Since this story was published, of course, evidence has been found for extensive quasi-neuronal communication among plants — but 100% predictive accuracy is not an essential criterion for science fiction.

The story interrogates, progressively, the very concepts of language and text. The ant's poetry, like a Dickinson poem or the translation of a Babylonian fragment, presents the problems of interpreting a conventional text. The Penguin article extends the language/text concept to a kinetic language — one of bodily motion, as in dance — and moves very quickly beyond that idea to the notion that the mind of an aquatic bird must, for evolutionary reasons, work differently from that of a fish or an aquatic mammal. As soon as the reader gets the point — perhaps even before it has sunk in — the essay drills down to the essential differences between species of penguins and the way each species's concerns influence thought and language. It finishes with a description of poetry offered in the cold and the dark by beings that move very slowly, so as not to dislodge the single egg that sits on each one's feet — a poetry written only in body heat. The Penguin specialist, after describing an expedition that would sit all winter in the Antarctic night to detect and interpret the poetry of the Emperor penguin, cheerily notes that there are still four places available (out of a possible five, perhaps?), and suggests that the reader might want to sign up now.

And the whole story is funny. (Did I mention it's funny? Boy, is it funny.) The voices of the scientists, each so different from one another, are hilarious, but gentle, parodies of human communications — the ways intelligently obsessive people impart information and enthusiasms to others. Even the heart-breaking parts are funny — the doomed ant, a formic Dickinson writing desperate poetry, with her feelers, on one seed after another, is both affecting and wacky, as is the existence of a Freudian interpreter. The ant's personal story is as unknowable as Sappho's, and the meaning of her poetry is as dependent as that of the Hittites on a translator's sincere but questionable extrapolation. How well does anyone know the internal life of another, of whatever species? It's a question that is both profound and, expressed in this context, extremely funny. In the second section, the emperor penguins, presumably male, crowded together in the dark, cradling eggs, composing poetry by sending whiffs of precious body-heat to one another, are touchingly funny — in their parallel with the production of human art from the cave to the present, and (to me anyway) in the implied visual: a bunch of guys standing around in the dark with eggs on their feet, doing their best to keep the species going.

The more I think about this story, the more amused I get: it is endlessly rewarding. Communication in the story, you'll notice, goes in only one direction. There is no indication that any of the other creatures are at all interested in understanding humans. The implications are that the universe is larger than humans, that yes, we can understand others, if not perfectly, and that all life, not just human, is funny and tragic. Even the capitalization of Ant and Penguin, in referring to the languages, strikes me as a comment on nationalism in English-language orthography.

In 1974, "The Author of the Acacia Seeds" absolutely blew me away, speaking directly to my writerly backbrain. It told me that the telling of complexly layered, multi-phasically imaginative stories was possible in genre science fiction. It didn't tell me how rare they were, or how difficult they were to write, but in 1974, what I needed to know was how high to set my aspiration.

An attempt at interpreting such a witty tale seems like a typically human effort to explain rather than communicate. Le Guin satirized, in the story itself, this very essay, and I realize now that she was making subtle fun of me before I had even read the story....

Thank you, Ursula, for all the epiphanies.

[Untitled]

KIM STANLEY ROBINSON

IT BEGAN FOR ME with some slim Ace paperbacks. *Planet of Exile, Rocannon's World, City of Illusions*. They all had travel in them, wilderness travel. People on foot, or carried by flying cats, or sailing, or cross-country skiing. Making their way across a landscape. I loved them for that. They were in a line with Edgar Pangborn and Jack Vance and Clifford Simak, a type of science fiction aware of the romance of other planets, aware also of human depths and the mystery of things. And these new books were especially knowing and sure, pitch perfect in both anthropological language and the rhythms of myth — they were poetry.

So I, like a lot of other people, was well set up for *The Left Hand of Darkness*. This book was everything that had come before and more. It had the travel and the mysterious beauty of the earlier Hainish novels, and then also it had its big metaphor, an image for us here and now which said: we are all just people. Ocassionally gender matters, but often it doesn't. There are roles we play. There are attributes we label masculine or feminine that have nothing to do with reproduction, but are qualities that shift around, both among and within people.

That powerful image of wholeness, combined with the great trek of Genly Ai and Estraven across the ice, created for me one of the best science fiction novels ever. From its time of publication until now, I like many others have put it forward as an exemplar of not only how good science fiction can be, but also how it can do things that other kinds of fiction can't.

And it changed the way I saw people, including myself. For some years I got to play that role we call "Mr. Mom," and as I lived it I understood it partly in terms learned from *The Left Hand of Darkness*. The king wasn't pregnant, but he sure did a lot of bottle feedings. Sometimes it would make me laugh.

Then I laughed again at *The Lathe of Heaven*, and read with awe *The Wind's Twelve Quarters*, and I recall very distinctly the cover and underweight heft of a Science Fiction Book Club edition of *The Dispossessed* that a friend lent me one day in 1975. I began to read it at my parents' house in my old room, and at some late hour reached what my wife and I would later call the Dickinson Point, by which we mean that moment when you realize you are going to have to finish a book even though it is already past midnight. I read through that night, on fire with the feeling that science fiction could do anything.

Later that same year I returned to UC San Diego to go to graduate school. I had given up on a Ph.D. program in Boston because of the climactic shock of my first-ever winter, and back at UCSD I quickly felt that I had made a mistake, even ruined my life. I was so bummed I told my new university acquaintances to call me Kim.

I had been to Clarion, however, and had sold a couple of stories, so I focused on my writing, and after a time adjusted. And then the literature department announced that Ursula K. Le Guin was going to be teaching on campus in the spring quarter of 1977. Maybe returning hadn't been such a mistake after all!

·

As I understand it, this was the first time Le Guin had been invited to teach at a university. The invitation was mainly the work of Professor Robert Elliott, who had written a book on utopia and was a fan of Le Guin's work. The plan was for her to come for the last month of the quarter, with my friend Lowry Pei teaching her classes until she arrived, after which he would team-teach with her. A good plan; Lowry is a great teacher, and he handled everything perfectly. By the time Le Guin arrived we were all very excited to have her with us.

She taught two classes, one on the literature of science fiction, the other a writing workshop. I took both of them.

The literature class was a seminar of about fifteen or twenty people. The class met on Tuesdays and Thursdays, and we were asked to read one novel per class, with two students making reports on that day's book, and the rest then discussing it. The novels Ursula assigned were *Hard To Be a God* by the Strugatski brothers, *Martian Time-Slip* by Philip K. Dick, *Camp Concentration* by Thomas M. Disch, *The Invincible* by Stanislaw Lem, *The Fifth Head of Cerberus* by Gene Wolfe, *The Dream Master* by Roger Zelazny, *The Exile Waiting* by Vonda N. McIntyre, and *And Strange at Ecbatan the Trees* by Michael Bishop. We also discussed at some length Italo Calvino's novels *The Non-Existent Knight*, *The Cloven Viscount*, and *The Baron in the Trees*, which I think were recent discoveries of Ursula's, and perhaps her addition to the reports. She led the discussions with a light touch, and an obvious pleasure in the books she had chosen.

In my report I joked that Number Five's name in *The Fifth Head of Cerberus* seemed to be "Gene Wolf," which made Ursula laugh. On the other hand, if one were to say something insulting about one of the books, as only a foolish young man would do, she could skewer one promptly and effectively.

She kept five hours of office hours a week, and I dropped by fairly often. It seemed to me that any time she spent alone during those hours would be time wasted.

In the writing class her method was mainly the workshop system developed at Clarion and Milford; I believe she had taught a week at Clarion West a year or two before. We wrote stories, turned in copies to her and all the other students, and commented on them as a group. She also gave us some in-class exercises, and made suggestions for kinds of stories to try outside of class. One in-class exercise was to write a brief story entirely in dialog. A suggestion for stories written outside of class was, "Set a story Elsewhere." Eventually Ursula turned in a story of her own to be workshopped, as did Lowry.

Ursula was very supportive of writing of all kinds, and as the month passed she helped us to cohere as a group of people who cared for one another, which is really the important thing in a workshop. I recall parties with her sitting on the floor. And I have a strong memory of her sitting immediately to my left when the class went to see the new movie *Star Wars*; we laughed our heads off. As a space-opera spoof it was even better than *Buck Rogers in the Twenty-fifth Century*.

At some time during the month I gave her a long mess of a novella, which I later sorted out as the third part of *Icehenge*. She dutifully read this and made what comments she could. That was a generous thing to do, given how much other reading she had; and she encouraged me in the best way possible. Write more, she told me. Finish more stories and see what happens.

There were people in the workshop writing excellent stories out of their own lives, heartfelt things that seemed to me to put science fiction to some ultimate existential questions. Why write science fiction at all, when people could say things so clearly and directly? What was the point? I talked to Ursula about these questions, and afterward pulled out a backpacking story I had started and abandoned two years earlier. Three friends in the high Sierra, one of them recovering from a head injury. The more I understood that the brain damage repair was both a science fiction device and an image for how I felt, the more "Ridge Running" became its own thing, separate from my trip while still relying on what I had done and seen up there.

"I like this one best of all your stories," Ursula said when the story was workshopped. You should think about doing more like this one.

That was an important moment for me.

At her going-away party I gave her a paperback of *The Dispossessed* to sign, and she signed it "To Kim/Stan Stim/Kan — you know who I mean. Love Ursula."

Since that time I have seldom seen Ursula. I've read her subsequent work with great pleasure, from *Malafrena* to *Lavinia*. Every once in a while we have corresponded a little; I have treasured her letters, and keep them in such a safe place that I can't find them anymore. Recently, when I have gotten to meet her for lunch in Portland, sometimes with Molly Gloss, it is a special occasion for me. I hope for more of them.

Then also, often through the years, when trying to explain what I do, talking about both science fiction and nature at once, and seeing on people's faces that they think I must be a hopelessly confused person, I have invoked Le Guin's name; and often they have nodded and said Oh, yes, now I see what you mean. I'm reminded of a moment in the film documenting Louis Armstrong's seventieth birthday party at the Newport Jazz Festival, when Dizzy Gillespie takes the mike and with hand on heart declares, "This person *invented my livelihood.*" It feels like that.

So happy birthday Ursula, with love and thanks from your Stan.

Dancing the World:
Landscape and Cosmology in Le Guin

LYNN ALDEN KENDALL

"I DON'T create worlds. I find them. They just come rising out of
my unconscious. Do you know the Indian stories about the Earth
Diver? An animal, usually a turtle, dives down to the bottom of the
sea, accidentally brings back some mud on his back, and sort of pats
it around until it becomes the mountains and the rocks and the
trees. I feel like that turtle."
    — URSULA K. LE GUIN[1]

The worlds that rise from Ursula K. Le Guin's unconscious range from
groves of great trees to rocky deserts to archipelagoes. Some are paradises
empty of animals, while others support complex and happy civilizations.
(Or unhappy ones.) Other writers in this book will surely discuss the
characters who people those worlds, who speak, work, dance, explore, and
suffer in ways that are recognizably human, even when the people were
born light-years away from Earth and with an alien biology.

The worlds themselves, however, are worth examining. Le Guin's
concern for "the shape and weight and fit of things" ("The Diary of the
Rose," p. 112) expresses itself in her world-building. Like Tolkien, like
the great Russian writers, Le Guin grounds her imagination in carefully
observed sensual detail, so even her wildest flights have the solid ring of
fact.

Furthermore, the natural history is not just a delightful detail but essential to her fiction. Le Guin consistently uses landscape as a mirror and metaphor of the story. In much of her work, the landscape goes beyond symbolic importance to take an active role in determining the events of the narrative.

In two of her stories, Le Guin shows how worlds are called forth. "The New Atlantis" is set in a future Portland after the sea level has risen and drowned much of the coast. ("There are oyster beds in Ghirardelli Square.") Belle, a violist, plays music that summons the world sunk beneath the sea:

> A huge, calling, yearning music from far away in the darkness, calling not to us. *Where are you? I am here.*
>
> Not to us.
>
> They were the voices of the great souls, the great lives, the lonely ones, the voyagers. Calling. Not often answered. *Where are you? Where have you gone?*

The New Atlantis awakens, becomes aware, and rises from the sea in response to Belle's music, which in turn is informed by her love for her husband Simon, and by Simon's work as a physicist.

In "The Pathways of Desire," a team of interplanetary anthropologists encounter a strangely familiar culture and language. The Young Ndif are an Edenic version of Earth teenagers, with plenty of sex but no babies. They occupy their time with competitions and hunting, but have little meaning in their lives. ("They all talk like Hemingway characters.") The Old Ndif, however, are developing a much more complex society with healing songs and sacred spaces.

"I would say that it seems that the Old Ndif are engaged in creating the world. Human beings do this primarily by means of language, music, and the dance."

— Ramchandra, in "The Pathways of Desire"

However, when one of the anthropologists is killed in a ritual duel, the other two anthropologists find genuine love expressed in meaningful sexuality. Then they discover that the whole world has been daydreamed, is being daydreamed, by a teenager presumably on Earth.

"Who dreamed the Earth? A greater dreamer than you or I, but we are the dreamer, Shakti, and the worlds will endure as long as our desire." [2]

The geographer of richly detailed imaginary worlds must have such worlds within her. The sea from which worlds rise is the sea within, the individual unconscious that ultimately leads to the collective unconscious.

Ursula K. Le Guin brings these worlds to life with uncommon skill, but the dancer is inseparable from the dance, as the style is from the story. The music of her writing is as refreshing and powerful as running water. Although not every one of her books is a masterpiece, she has never let a bad sentence reach print. The description of the Immanent Grove in *The Other Wind* moved me to tears with its sheer beauty.

Another essential element of her cosmology is her generous, great-hearted vision of persons and peoples of all kinds, cultures, colors, shapes, genders. She can be fair to people with dragon's wings, people whose wings fail, people who decide never to use their wings. She depicts arrogance, anger, and madness at times; her characters can be stubborn and self-deceived. They can do damage to the balance of the world. But there is remarkably little pettiness or spite in the author's imagination, and a great deal of love.

She peoples her worlds with believable characters, some of whom I love like my own family. This is not an exaggeration; I married a man uncommonly like Itale Sorde in his devotion to home, his intelligence, his interest in justice. (It's not surprising that he was from a Central European family; Orsinia's rich culture is rooted in the glories of the kingdoms east of Germany.) The hoarse, scarred, yet powerful survivor Tehanu is both a realistic and an inspirational figure, but the reader never forgets that Tehanu is also a badly abused child with unspeakable memories.

As time has passed, Le Guin's worlds have become more complex, more inclusive, and more beautiful. The author's increasing wisdom had its roots in an uncommon upbringing (one that might be described as the patriarchy at its very best, loving, intellectual, liberal) and might well never have grown beyond that well-tended garden. But Le Guin has the courage to keep learning. Over time she has come to embrace new, radical, disturbing ideas and begun to see the world from the point of view of the poor and the powerless.

Very few people have the honesty, toughness, and generosity to admit their blind spots and try to correct them in the ways Le Guin has done. To admit the flaws and missed chances of one's most famous and honored work is almost unprecedented, yet Le Guin has done it with both *The Left Hand of Darkness* and the Earthsea books.

Revisioning the Earthsea cycle is a particularly impressive feat of imagination. Reading the series beginning to end, as I recently did, I saw the whole story unscroll like a tapestry. Seen in that light, it works. It coheres. It turns from its original focus and reaches out to embrace everyone. The final vision, deeper, burnished, retains the artistic integrity of the much-loved trilogy, while enhancing and broadening its message. The threads that become *The Other Wind* — which may be her finest work — were implicit in *A Wizard of Earthsea.*

I come back again and again to Le Guin's stories and novels, drawn by the peace and majesty of her trees on their steep sunlit hillsides, to kneel and drink at the creeks of her worlds. Even her alien planets are richly imagined. Many are places I'd like to live.

One of the roles of the artist is to show us the world in a way we haven't seen before. Ursula K. Le Guin shows us our dreams, our failures, our own world, its landscapes as well as its people, and she translates it for us. She herself may be what she described in "The Author of the Acacia Seeds" as:

> the first geolinguist, who, ignoring the delicate, transient lyrics of the lichen, will read beneath it the still less communicative, still more passive, wholly atemporal, cold, volcanic poetry of the rocks: each one a word spoken, how long ago, by the earth itself, in the immense solitude, the immenser community, of space.

NOTES:

1. Fadiman, Anne. "Ursula K. Le Guin: voyager to the inner land." *Life* 9 (April 1986): 23(3). General OneFile. Gale. ALAMEDA COUNTY LIBRARY SYSTEM. 6 Sept. 2009: *find.galegroup.com/gps/start.do?prodId=IPS*

2. I've always suspected that this story is a gentle bop to the head of Robert Heinlein. Bob, the slain anthropologist, is a big, handsome blond man who ends up participating in the unfettered, meaningless sexuality of the young Ndif, which bears a painfully close resemblance to the sexual behavior of many Heinlein characters.

The Nobies' Story

BRIAN ATTEBERY

THEY MET at Thurman Street more than two years before their first book together, and there, calling themselves after the project as most editorial crews did, become the Nobies, short for *Norton Book of Science Fiction*.

That's a slightly reworded version of Ursula K. Le Guin's "The Shobies' Story"(1990), about a mixed team of explorers trying out an unpredictable new form of instantaneous transport, or "transilience." The Shobies were very much on my mind as I headed off to Portland in early fall of 1991 to meet with Le Guin and Karen Joy Fowler. Ursula was our captain. It was she to whom Norton editor Dan Conaway had pitched the idea of doing a volume in their "Norton Book of" series, like the *Norton Book of Friendship*, edited by Eudora Welty. Clever Dan had noticed that his trade division had created a back door for a science-fiction volume even though the textbook division had refused for years to consider any sort of official Norton Anthology of the genre. Ursula was intrigued but wanted a crew, and suggested two co-editors, both of whom leaped at the chance.

Karen and I had never met. Her first novel, *Sarah Canary*, was just about to come out. I was finishing a book called *Strategies of Fantasy*. Ursula spotted possibilities in the two of us and our work and decided we would make a congenial team, so here we were gathering at the Le Guin house for a preliminary planning session, or what the people in Le Guin's science-fictional universe call *iseye*:

> The word is Hainish and means "making a beginning together," or "beginning to be together," or used technically, "the period of time and area of space in which a group forms if it is going to form." ("The Shobies' Story," 75)

Our iseye weekend started with tea and introductions and proceeded to long conversations about what we might do with this amazing opportunity. We each approached from a different perspective: Karen as a working writer relatively new to the field but tuned in to its most exciting current work; me as a scholar accustomed to thinking in terms of genre history and teaching practices; Ursula as — well, as Ursula K. Le Guin, exemplar of the genre's coming-of-age as a literary mode. We were all a bit intimidated by the task. Ursula had not been thinking much about science fiction for a few years, though she was just about to shake up the fantasy genre with *Tehanu*, her brilliant reimagining of the world of Earthsea. Karen and I were unsure of one another and (I'm guessing) both nervous about working with one of our idols. We had guidelines from Dan Conaway about word counts and contracts, but very little in the way of specific advice on selection and arrangement of the stories.

> They talked, as human beings do, about what they didn't know (76).

Over tea and cookies, we talked about our backgrounds, our families, and our personal journeys into speculative literature. We found common ground in being Westerners, parents (a particular preoccupation for me at the time, with a toddler and another child on the way), professors' kids, environmental activists, lovers of the odd and offbeat. With Ursula's deft guidance, Karen and I began to tune into one another's senses of humor. (The Fowler wit was not yet famous.) We all began to understand our editorial task as the construction of a new story about science fiction, one that would not necessarily contradict but would certainly re-position earlier stories about the field.

Here are some of the stories about science fiction.

Science fiction is a form of adventure writing that started in the pulp magazines of the early twentieth century, reached its peak in the 1940s, and went bad in the 1970s when women and literary types got involved.

Science fiction is Sci-Fi: spectacular cinematic scenes of weird environments and high-tech gadgets without a lot of human involvement. It retells old plots from Westerns and detective stories, but with more explosions.

Science fiction is a collection of utopian tracts and satires with a thin thread of plot. The best science fiction is European: Cyrano de Bergerac, Jonathan Swift, Jules Verne, H. G. Wells, J. G. Ballard, Stanislaw Lem.

Science fiction is American manifest destiny turned outward to the stars. Real SF is optimistic and problem-solving, with a white male engineer at the center of the action.

Science fiction is comic books in prose: a subliterature suitable to 12-year-olds and for those who have never grown past that level of maturity. This version of the story has even been told, oddly enough, by some people within the field.

These stories are all true. They have all been told many times, in the form of book reviews, encyclopedias, convention panels, classroom lectures, and — most relevant to our purposes — anthologies.

They are also all false. They leave out whatever doesn't fit the pattern, as all histories do. In our conversations, Ursula, Karen, and I discovered that we could not find within any of the standard stories a place for ourselves and our encounters with the genre. Over a weekend together, we compared notes, lists, and experiences, trying to fit them together into a coherent narrative.

Karen's story has been told elsewhere (including a version in her novel *The Jane Austen Book Club*) — it has to do with coming to science fiction late and almost accidentally (to impress a date), but also being introduced by way of the very best work of the 1960s and '70s, including Le Guin's.

My story was about finding the one shelf of science fiction in our small Carnegie Library (in the adult section, so that I had to talk my father or my sister into checking books out for me until I reached eighth grade and could get my own adult library card). Among the few books on that shelf were anthologies in which I found the rich and strange worlds of, among others, Theodore Sturgeon, Cordwainer Smith, Lewis Padgett (who I didn't know for years was really C. L. Moore and Henry Kuttner writing together). These stories got me hooked; then, around the time when I might have lost interest, along came the paperback revolution, and I was drawn in all over again by Roger Zelazny, Joanna Russ, Samuel R. Delany, and Ursula K. Le Guin. I had a few friends who shared my interest, but I never found any fan groups, attended any conventions, or had a teacher who encouraged my interest as a legitimate literary study. That last was true all the way up to graduate school, when I encountered Robert Scholes.

Ursula's story came in several parts: early reading like mine, but in a different and gaudier era (*Amazing Stories* rather than *Galaxy Readers*); a return to the field when she found that the stories she wanted to write could be directed toward a science-fiction readership; joining a conversation of writers and scholars who were remaking the genre into a more ambitious version of itself in the '70s.

Out of all that, we constructed a narrative that we thought had never been articulated clearly. It was the story of science fiction's maturity. Hence, we decided to start our anthology in 1960 and go up to the present. 1960 was an arbitrary date — there were plenty of signs of maturation in the previous decade, and plenty of half-baked stuff afterward. The date worked, though, because it freed us from having to find a starting point (*Frankenstein?* Poe? Wells? Gernsback?) or reprint the old chestnuts. Besides, there were other historical anthologies available, such as James Gunn's excellent *Road to Science Fiction.*

Our present was, we decided, 1990. That was the flaw in our plan: as soon as we started choosing stories, we found ourselves regretting the ending date, since new and wonderful fiction was appearing monthly. By now, 1990 seems almost quaint. However, we did do a pretty good job of predicting the future by including many of the most interesting writers of the subsequent decades: John Kessel, Molly Gloss, Eleanor Arnason, Eileen Gunn, James Patrick Kelly, and Kim Stanley Robinson, to name just a few.

We also limited ourselves to English-language fiction from North America, for reasons of space and time. We already knew we were going to have to leave out wonderful stuff, and we also knew how much we didn't know about the past thirty years of science-fiction history, so we simplified our task by limiting our coverage to less than one half of one hemisphere — no francophone Canadian, nothing from Mexico or Central America or the Caribbean. And no excerpts from novels, although we fudged by finding a section of Russ's *The Female Man* that was published as a separate story first. None of these decisions is particularly defensible, except that we could not do otherwise and get through the task.

> As regards the churten process, they knew that it was supposed to effectuate their transilience to a solar system seventeen light-years from Ve Port without temporal interval; but nobody, anywhere, knew what they were doing. (89)

So we set about to tell how science fiction, or an almost manageable subset of it, had become a complex, elegant, funny, harrowing body of work that was not identical to the literary mainstream but was in no way inferior to it. That was where we wanted to end up. Getting there was another matter. Some of it was easy: we could each name a dozen writers we absolutely had to include, and our dozens almost coincided. We remembered stories we had read decades earlier that still colored our vision — some of those had to be in the anthology. Other choices were tough: go for the hot new writer or the neglected master? Pick someone's best-known work at the cost of turning him or her into a one-story writer? Represent every trend and trope or go for the most effective without worrying about balance?

We didn't spend the whole weekend poring over lists and charts. We had lunch, fixed by Charles Le Guin and including tomatoes from his garden. I remember one or two expeditions to downtown Portland, to Powell's and Great Northwest Books. We delved through back shelves for old anthologies and author collections, rediscovering half-forgotten old favorites like Edgar Pangborn and Margaret St. Clair (who didn't make it into the *Norton Book*) and James Schmitz and Zenna Henderson (who did). We came back to Ursula's house with sacks of paperbacks to divvy up. We assigned ourselves tasks: you go through these "best of the year" volumes and flag stories we should all look at; you locate something by this or that neglected author; I'll try to find a good late work by Blish or Sturgeon; we'll all pick a couple of under-anthologized pieces by Philip K. Dick or Samuel R. Delany.

> It was like we were still in the *Shoby* at Ve Port just waiting before we went into NAFAL flight. But it was like we were at the brown planet too. At the same time. And one of them was just pretend, and the other one wasn't, but I didn't know which. (103)

I think we actually spent some of our time reading, as a break from talking and as a start toward imagining the finished volume. One of us might be sitting in a chair on the deck, looking out at Charles's beautiful yard and distant Mt. St. Helens while simultaneously enduring the endless agonies of falling into a black hole. Another might be encountering Howard Waldrop's funny and tragic version of eighteenth century science from the vantage point of a window seat in Ursula's living room. All readers know that different spaces and times can overlie one another. That weekend in that house on Thurman Street was a particular point of convergence for alternative realities and infinite reaches of space. The three of us created a rhythm of voyaging separately and returning to tell tales, and we were to continue the pattern for the next months by telephone and post. At the end of the weekend, we went our separate ways and yet never left the imagined space we had created.

We read, and Xeroxed, and mailed, and argued, and reconvened in person two or three times. Eventually we had a table of contents. We proofread and compiled author biographies and identified key readers and reviewers. We met in Florida to unveil our plans at the International Conference on the Fantastic in the Arts, and again in Berkeley to launch our craft. We corresponded with delighted authors who were included, and miffed ones who weren't (and undoubtedly should have been). We snorted at inept reviewers (some of whom didn't seem to read beyond the title page and introduction) and admired the insights of abler ones. We shared book suggestions and family anecdotes, like the story of a picnic at which Charles Le Guin pulled my daughter out of the Willamette River.

Now almost twenty years later, I am continually surprised and delighted to find that I can count Karen and Ursula as friends, and that the story we ended up telling has found listeners around the world. It still isn't the only story about science fiction, and it shouldn't be. But it is a wonderful story because it tells about a genre of possibilities: a genre that invites the voices of people from different cultural backgrounds and genders and sexualities and races to explore what it means to live in a technologically mediated reality and a scientifically conceived universe that is also a world of myth and mystery. Our captain urged us in those directions, and the crew was happy to follow. We had learned from Ursula K. Le Guin that the story one chooses to tell determines the reality one ends up in.

"We need to know what's — real — what happened, whether any-thing happened —" Tai gestured at the cave of firelight around them and the dark beyond it. "Where are we? Are we here? Where is here? What's the story?" (102)

Le Guin, Ursula K. "The Shobies' Story." *A Fisherman of the Inland Sea.* New York: HarperCollins, 1994. 75–105.

The Word For World Is Forest

GWYNETH JONES

WHEN I first encountered US feminist science fiction, many years ago, two books made a special impact on me: *The Left Hand Of Darkness*, by Ursula K. Le Guin, and *The Female Man*, by Joanna Russ. It wasn't so much the sexual politics…in fact, I'd say the *sexual politics* of the outstanding feminist sf novels of those days were secondary for me, and for many readers. We were already aware of feminism, it seemed a normal topic of discussion. The impact was artistic. I loved the stylistic freedoms in these two books; the innovative use of real science, real politics, and familiar science-fiction tropes. Here was science and sci-fi not just used as dress-up for serious ideas, but fully integrated with those ideas. I thought *The Left Hand Of Darkness* was the most beautiful, most poetic sf I'd ever read (still do).

The Word For World Is Forest came later. I didn't read it until I came back to the UK after spending time in South East Asia. I was fascinated by the Athsheans, and the real world anthropology "synchronicity" reported in the foreword (in the Granada UK paperback, 1980). I'd been living in Singapore, travelling around Indonesia, making up stories about far-future psychic South East Asians, but I'd never heard of the Senoi and their dreamtime culture. Whatever we "invent" about strange human cultures, we have to find in our own minds: maybe we couldn't dream it if it weren't potentially real; real somewhere, somewhen. I did not read the story as "preaching" against the Vietnam war, not at all, possibly because by the time I read *The Word For World Is Forest* that war was over. Maybe I'd have felt differently if the original title of the 1972 story ("The Little Green Men") had been retained, but I don't think so. I think at its heart this was always a story about the rape of Earth, not about US imperialism in the jungle.

For the record, in case you don't know: this is the cautionary tale of an expedition from Earth, with somewhat shaky permissions to remove a massive quantity of hardwood from a planet where the natives have been wrongly categorised as not quite sentient. The Expedition, controlled by the military, has seriously overstepped the mark, and fallen into corruption. They are destroying the ecosystem and enslaving the unfortunate locals. There's routine brutality, there've been incidents of firebombing, rape, and torture. There's now a shady plan to turn "New Tahiti" into a permanent colony, for which purpose comfort girls and colony "brides" have been imported. The bad guy is called Captain Davidson, his foil is a Captain Lyubov, a gentle scientist with a make-believe military rank, who has made at least one dear friend among the Athsheans. But he couldn't stop his friend's wife from being raped by Davidson and dying of her injuries... The locals are physically small and slight, their mode of experiencing reality is different from ours and, crucially, they have no concept of organised violence. They're going to have to learn, and it won't be pretty.

I didn't find the blind, rapacious villainy of Captain Davidson overdone. Maybe he's more candid than such figures generally are, in real life: but of course he exists (look around you), and he's surrounded by more nuanced characters: ineffective and helpless for nuanced reasons; spoiled in subtle, tragic ways by violence. There are distant voices of benign authority who just don't understand (until too late) what people like Davidson are capable of. There are no simplistic good guys.

Reading the book again, in 2009, I notice, again, that the forest mourned in these pages is not the Vietnamese jungle. This is temperate zone forest, maybe the mossy, damp forests of the northwestern US seaboard; populated by trees with familiar names, pine, oak, walnut, chestnut, fir, apple:

> All the colours of rust and sunset, brown-reds and pale greens, changed ceaselessly in the long leaves as the wind blew. The roots of the copper willows were moss green down by the running water, which like the wind moved slowly with many soft eddies and seeming pauses... (27)

Of course there's a science-fiction explanation. The alien planet was "seeded" with the human race and the vegetation of Earth a million years ago by the Hain: the Elder Race. The humans died out, the trees prospered. But the message that the locus of destruction is close to home is hard to miss. Harder still now, after forty years of grief and loss for the people of Earth's forests, and for the defenders of the green world. The raw anger seems entirely justified, given the way the evidence is mounting up: evidence that the word for world *is* forest, and without the forests, unless we can restore the forests, there may be nothing left of the living world.

The Word For World is Forest does what serious science fiction does best. It shows us our own world, made strange and familiar: makes us feel the beauty and mystery of this totally extraordinary (one of a kind, you know) planet. And rails against abuses, not in polemic speeches, but through the focused lens of a simple, tragic drama. It's a minor masterpiece.

Ursula K. Le Guin: Mutinous Navigator

VONDA N. MCINTYRE

FIRST OF ALL, she likes robot toys.

And she's the wisest person I've ever met.

The two factors aren't unrelated. Her stories, from "The Author of the Acacia Seeds and Other Extracts from the *Journal of the Association of Therolinguistics*" to "Bunditsu: The Art of Cat Arranging," reflect her humor and her wisdom. She knows that the world can be funny as well as sad, pedestrian as well as magical, and that we're connected to the humor and the magic as well as to the sadness and the pain.

While I was writing this introduction, I laughed out loud at the dedication to "Ether, OR" — "To the Narrative Americans."

I smiled all the way through the solstice chant from "Winter Solstice Ritual for the Pacific Northwest":

> It is holy in the east.
> It is holy in the north.
> It is holy in the west.
> It is holy in the south.
> Up above it is holy.
> Down below it is holy.
> It is holy in the middle and around the outsides.
> It is holy in all the crevices and little sticking-out bits.
> It is holy in all the parts I have forgotten.

Between the toes and behind the ears it is holy.
Along the selvedges and hems and seams and gussets it is holy.
It is holy between 2:30 and 4 and even in prime time.
It is fairly generally and as a more or less continuous thing holy.

— and then I reread "Neko at Twenty" and burst into tears:

Opaque and luminous gaze
fixed on longer than a cat can live...

I've been privileged to know Ursula for more than half my life. When I had known her for ten minutes, and though I knew she hadn't taught fiction writing before, I begged her to teach at a workshop I was helping organize. Twenty-five years later, organizing another workshop, I spent the first ten minutes on the job asking her to teach at it.

(By the way, she said "Yes" both times, and she was wonderful both times. And at the workshops in between, she was fairly generally and as a more or less continuous thing, wonderful.)

She's the best teacher I've ever seen: witty, generous, gentle, truthful. Though she has strong and unique ideas about fiction, rather than bully new writers into agreeing with her and mimicking her, she encourages them to blaze their own trails. The book she based on her workshop experience, *Steering the Craft*, has the subtitle, "Exercises and Discussions on Story Writing for the Lone Navigator or the Mutinous Crew."

She is mutinous herself on occasion, and rather dangerous. She isn't afraid to change her mind, and to admit to changing her mind, and to discuss changing her mind. I think she likes the way this adds a slightly

chaotic wobble to the balance of her life…not to mention to the procla-
mations of critics.

Rather that trying to suppress her mutinous crews, she cherishes them.
She introduces her students to new ways of looking at the world and at
their fiction. She's certainly done that for me, as well as introducing me
to the magical Olympic rain forest, the severe and beautiful and utterly
indifferent Oregon desert, and the Southwest. She introduced me to the
music of Bruce Springsteen. She even introduced me to the New Mexico
State Crustacean.

(Have you noticed those? They're overrunning the state. They've made
it to the Northwest, too — they're about four feet high, three feet wide,
bright orange with reflective stripes, and they line up in roadways. She
and I ranged through Los Alamos taking pictures of them one afternoon,
for a treatise on the Crustaceans' natural history. I believe the inhabitants
thought we were atom bomb spies. They might also have thought we were
making free with the nitrous oxide, as we were laughing like loons every
time we found a new Crustacean subspecies.)

She's mutinous about her self-descriptions, as well. Mutinous and
dangerously unpopular. She uses the F-word — feminist — all the time.
About herself. Despite some efforts in the literary mainstream to drag her
out of the science fiction field — I think they think she is too good for us,
and sometimes I think they might be right…but then again I think she's
too good for them, too — she always describes herself, first and foremost,
as a *science* fiction writer.

She's also not afraid to use the epithet "politically correct," though to be
sure she uses it in its original sense of respecting other peoples' differing
points of view.

Ursula's life reflects her wisdom and her humor, just as her stories do. She once said to me, "One person can't excel at two simultaneous careers, but two people can successfully share three." She and her husband Charles share three careers: he is an historian, she a fiction writer, and they both are parents, of three wonderful and completely different adult children. The very first time I ever visited the Le Guins, I noticed that while Ursula and Charles were definitely the parents, and Elisabeth, Caroline, and Theo were the children, the parents always spoke to the children as fellow human beings. Ursula and Charles excel at three careers. Four, actually, now that they are grandparents.

I don't know if you can count friendship as a career, but they are pretty darned good at that, too.

One last thing. Ursula isn't perfect. And she wouldn't even like it if I claimed she was. But this isn't a roast, it's a celebration. So I'm not going to tell you any ways she isn't perfect. I'm only going to celebrate her, and to invite you to celebrate with me.

WRITTEN FOR THE PRESENTATION OF THE
BUMBERSHOOT AWARD TO URSULA K. LE GUIN.

Ursula's Eightieth

A Sonnet Upon it

KAREN JOY FOWLER

SUNRISE at the edge of the world. We dance,
the dog and I (the dog deadweight). We hear
the cri de coeur of seals, the "ur, ur, ur"
of Ursula. The morning sun advances.

Dazzled sea and rock below. Above
me, lines of pelicans, a cloud of gulls
unlock the air with joyful aerials.
We celebrate! It is the birthday of

the worlds of Omelas, Urras, Gethen,
O, of Rocannon and the Ansarac,
and more. All are very far away from
anywhere, yet each one holds this lesson:
that, wander where you will, (or even walk
away) and still you're always coming home.

Happy birthday!

Thank you, Ursula

MJ HARDMAN

IT HAS been interesting to learn that most of fandom seems to have grown up reading SF. I did not even learn of the existence of the field until I was already a full professor. Through literature classes I learned of "utopias" (like Thomas More's[1]), and in second grade I had discovered *Alice in Wonderland* and *Through the Looking Glass*,[2] but did not know that this was "fantasy" until many decades later.

My children did drag me into *Star Trek*, but only in the reruns in the late seventies. Then there was *Star Wars*, and, lo and behold, Quechua was used for the alien language in the bar scene. At the time we were teaching the Aymara language at the University of Florida.[3] The two languages are not related, but they are both spoken in the Andes, and most people don't know anything about them anyway. I was asked by the local SF club to give a talk about the Quechua in that scene; that invitation suddenly made the field of SF present for me. Since I had written a Quechua grammar way back when and since my teaching assistant at that time also knew some Quechua, we did give the presentation — the language used is a quite well known poem with the nonexotic parts excised. As a thank you, the club gave me *A Wizard of Earthsea* by Ursula K. Le Guin:[4] my very first SF book and my real introduction to the whole SF field. I, naturally, assumed that this was a typical SF book; I immediately went on to read Tiptree (and after reading the first story and going back for more I learned she had just been outed), Joanna Russ and Octavia Butler. It was only much later that I learned that the field was supposed to be "masculine." Hmmm. Didn't look that way to me, as I worked my way through Le Guin's even then impressive bibliography.

Eventually, since I was hooked, I did go back and read the "golden age" works. I don't know what I might have thought had I read the works as a child; I know that as an adult they certainly did not work for me, though I do not regret reading what are indeed the historical works of the field; this allows me to understand and value the courage and genius that give to me the magnificent reading that I have today at my fingertips, and, on this occasion to say thank you to Ursula K. Le Guin.

I first had the honor of meeting Ursula at WisCon when she gave the amazing special guest of honor speech that starts with "I am a man." Exquisite. It immediately became required reading for my students.[5] Quite a number of the works from her extensive bibliography have found their way onto my syllabi, not only for Linguistics and Science Fiction, but also for the language and culture/gender/violence courses.[6] Quite obviously, *The Left Hand of Darkness* is such a book, even in its first edition, but of great value for my students are the appendices for the 25th anniversary edition[7] where she revisits her earlier work and presents one chapter with three different sets of pronouns. The power of language use becomes beautifully obvious as students reflect on their own reactions to the text. Language does matter.

In 2003 one of my honors students, Heather Pippin, gave an academic paper at WisCon, "Needlecrafting as a Generative Metaphor in Feminist Science Fiction," drawing on the work of Ursula K. Le Guin, Suzette Haden Elgin, and Élisabeth Vonarburg. All three authors were in the audience for her paper. It was her very first academic paper; that she could be so honored was impressive indeed, being able to meet and speak with those whose works she so admired.

But the work that I would like to discuss here in some detail is *Always Coming Home*.[8] This masterpiece rewards rereading, works for several classes, and remains on my recommendation list for all who consult me.

About the same time that I was discovering the existence of sf I was also developing my theoretical concept of the Linguistic Postulate.[9] I have defined the Linguistic Postulate as a theme or motif that can be found in almost all the sentences of a language, a feature that is used repeatedly by the speakers of the language to organize the universe. The Postulates are grammatical features of the language with cultural echoes that are considered by the native speakers as "natural," as part of being human. Indeed, we all acquire such postulates as we acquire our native language/society/culture as a single complex structure. "The language," when used to refer to a specific, always refers to a complex linguistic/social/cultural construct at a particular moment in time/space that therefore constrains even as it permits the ongoingness of that moment. However, as contradictory as this seems, it is also possible to say anything in any language.[10] All languages can encompass the totality of human experience. How easily a given "language" does so, how efficiently, how often which experiences are encoded, varies enormously and constitutes the life work of many a linguist.

My original purpose in developing the theory was to be able to discuss that which I had found in the grammar and culture of the Jaqi languages, grammatical structures and cultural patterns that I found fascinating and liberating to me personally. I thought that what I found would be of wide interest. It was not. I found two problems: when I start to discuss grammar, folks go to sleep; that one I learned to work around, including the development of the theoretical construct of the Linguistic Postulate. The second turned out to be far more difficult. The Postulates of any given language/culture/society construct turn out to be so strong that convincing anyone that they are not so elsewhere becomes like leaping high walls indeed. I was surprised, shocked, and continue to be. What I had found among the Jaqi was not canon; it could not be admitted.

As an example, just this summer in Perú a person with power to make or break bilingual education for the Jaqaru language, which at this moment is very very threatened, has just now, after hearing me lecture in person, come to understand something I wrote, and he read, in 1972.[11] Only now, in 2009, could I be heard, with, we surely hope, good consequences for allowing the children of Tupe to read and write in their own language before it is gone, not only from them but from all of us as a human race as well.

Materials for children must incorporate and respect the Postulates of their own language/culture/society construct or they will not learn it or they will reject the language materials as fallacious (which did happen). Materials translated directly (not as a great art, which can be done and is a different issue) from one language to another carry with them the postulates of the original language; they are not appropriate materials for elementary school (think of some of the translated instructions you've found with electronics products). This is imperialism or colonialism (or sloppy translating); it is not creativity in language. If all that is available is such inauthentic text, because the powers that be cannot imagine a language without their own Postulates, then the language is doomed, in today's world of globalization.[12]

Circumstances led me to turn the lens back to my own language, out of which I developed the related theoretical construct of Derivational Thinking.[13] It takes me nearly three months to lead some students to see the postulates of their own language, let alone come to appreciate those of another, or even believe that it can be otherwise.[14]

One of the great joys for me is that I come to SF to find places where the current ties of language/society/culture are defied within the language by speakers of the language, creatively. Within feminist SF many would defy the sexist construction of our language/society/culture, some more successfully than others. Ursula was doing exactly that in *The Left Hand of Darkness*, as I commented above.

As a linguist, I put all of this into academese, appropriately, but I have also been working to present my material to an audience that does not necessarily know linguistics. Within my courses I present the Linguistic Postulates of English within the theoretical construct of Derivational Thinking (see above), those grammatical structures that pair with our cultural structures and that sabotage many of our highly desirable principles, like equality. One of these, clearly, is sexism. Another is hierarchy. As stated above, "the language" normally refers to a specific time/place; for that definition what I present is absolutely true, frequently to the great shock of those in my class. Simultaneously, it is possible to do otherwise because all languages are open systems; as I stated above, it is possible to say all things in any language, though what you must say, what is difficult to say, what will take you a very long time to say, and what you can say conveniently varies enormously.

In *Always Coming Home*, Ursula shows us that we can, yes, use English in ways that are not hierarchical and that are not sexist and where number belongs only to counting not to ranking. In my academese, she writes a novel in English without using Derivational Thinking — a beautiful reply to those who ask me "What can we do about it?"

We start with a carrier novel, one that may be read in a linear way, but the content isn't linear, or it may be read in any number of ways. I have read it cover to cover, but I have reread it in several ways. I now have a favorite way that works well with students: they start with the three Stone-Telling sections, and then they read the rest in what appears to be a "jumping around" way, thus learning the language/culture of the Kesh (and they also listen to the tape/disc), and then they reread the three Stone-Telling sections. At that point they finally perceive the postulates of the Kesh; it makes sense. The poem from page 313 of the book is posted outside my office door and that is one of the pieces we read aloud in class. For us, it is a classic:

> Like and different are quickening words,
> Brooding and hatching.
> Better and worse are eggsucking words,
> They leave only the shell.

Those few words put into beauty the problem with the hierarchy postulate of English. Thanks to *Always Coming Home*, I can say to my students that no, you do not have to allow your language to control you; you can also take your language and work with it and allow it to support the culture/society that you wish to construct, understanding that to do so all three elements — language/society/culture — must walk together.

Students' reactions are quite fascinating. There is always the stray student who doesn't quite understand the first sentence, with the absolutely marvelous verb phrase: "The people in this book *might be going to have lived* a long, long time ago in Southern California" (italics added). They will actually believe that the book IS a translation and ask me where the author got the original! Others understand the sentence, but believe that the author has done a superb job in mimicking a translation because it is so hard to read; it "sounds" like a foreign language. For most they find the language "strange," but adjust after not too many pages, and then find it "normal." As we all know, this is one of the great pleasures of SF. We enter into the "strange" and it becomes "normal." And the students become vicarious participants in a culture where the postulates are the unity of all living beings, where number is not an issue, where competition and violence is for children, and where the Linguistics Postulates of their own language are not used, but rather English is used beautifully and creatively to step aside from such structures and create others.

The most recent encounter I had with Ursula, also at WisCon, was a breakfast in the Governor's Club Lounge. Thank you, Ursula, for the company and the conversation; it is such a joy to find that one is not alone in attitudes towards clustering or grouping in the matter of awards, that the recognition of merit need not be (and seldom is) a single point; indeed that focus on singularity leaves works and people that deserve recognition as "losers." We need not do that, say some of us.

The power of SF, for me, is in the possibilities it shows for the use of language to construct the unknown and thus to open the potential for us to create for ourselves our language/society/culture as we would like it to be.

Thank you, Intrumo, for all the pleasure you have given me and for all the material you have provided for my students. I am glad that you are here among us. May you be so for a long long time yet.

NOTES:

1 Saint Thomas More. Utopia. 1516. (Latin: *Dē optimō reī pūblicae statū dēque novā īnsulā Ūtopiā*)

2 Carroll, Lewis. *Alice's Adventures in Wonderland* and *Through the Looking Glass*, with 86 original illustrations by John Tenniel. Chicago/New York: M.A. Donohue & Co. N.D. [a book I still own, nearly seven decades later].

3 *at.ufl.edu/~hardman-grove/almp/almp.html*; more general information available on my mainpage *at.ufl.edu/~hardman-grove/*, since Aymara is one of the three Jaqi languages; detailed information, actually a full two-year college course, is available at *aymara.ufl.edu/*.

4 Le Guin, Ursula K. *A Wizard of Earthsea*. Boston, MA: Parnassus/ Houghton Mifflin 1968; New York: Ace 1970; New York: Atheneum 1991.

5 First from my program book (1996) and later in its published version: "Introducing Myself." *The Wave in the Mind*, Boston, MA: Shambhala, 2004.

6 The recent list can be gleaned from looking through the syllabi on the left-hand side of my website *at.ufl.edu/~hardman-grove/*; many other works were used earlier, but adding to a course syllabus also means subtracting.

7 Le Guin, Ursula K. *The Left Hand of Darkness*. New York: Walker & Co, 1994.

8 Le Guin, Ursula K. *Always Coming Home*. Berkeley, CA: University of California Press, 2001.

9 Hardman, M.J. "Linguistics Postulates and Applied Anthropological Linguistics," in *Papers on Linguistics and Child Language*, Ruth Hirsch Weir Memorial Volume, Editors Honsa & Hardman. The Hague: Mouton, 1978.

10 For a long and thorough discussion of this apparent contradiction I recommend Suzette Haden Elgin's *Language Imperative*, Cambridge, MA: Perseus Books, 2000.

11 Hardman, M.J. "Postulados lingüísticos del idioma Aymara," in *Reto del Multilinguismo en el Perú*, Editor Alberto Escobar. Lima, Perú: IEP, 1972.

12 A recent book that discusses this loss is *Dying Words: Endangered Languages and What They Have to Tell Us* by Nicholas Evans (Oxford: Blackwell, 2009).

13 There is a (not really updated) bibliography on my webpage *at.ufl. edu/~hardman-grove/* on the right; some of the articles themselves are under "resources" on the left. A good place to start is 1993 "Gender Through the Levels," in *Women and Language* Vol xvi no. 2 pp 42–49, or 1996 "The Sexist Circuits of English," *The Humanist* March/April 1996 pp 25–32.

14 A number of students have used the lens of Linguistic Postulates to look at other languages; the construct of Derivational Thinking has been used to take a close look at a number of aspects of the local (usa and/or university) culture as well.

Four Contributions from Beyon'Dusa

BEYON'DUSA is an artists' collective, five wild wimmin writing and living these times together, no matter what, since 1999 and goin' strong. Andrea Hairston, Ama Patterson, Pan Morigan, Sheree Renée Thomas, and Liz Roberts.

We honor a great artist who has sustained and transformed a tradition by adding to it.

Beyon'Dusa offers:

> ANDREA HAIRSTON — the first chapter of *Will Do Magic*
> *For Small Change*, a novel in progress, with foreword
> SHEREE R. THOMAS — "Touch," a short story
> AMA PATTERSON — "Seamonsters," a short story, with foreword
> PAN MORIGAN — "The Heart of the Song," a short story, with
> afterword

❦ I FIRST READ *The Dispossessed* in the '70s — thirty-five years ago — and my world changed. At the time, instead of using my gifts, voice, or powers to become a scientist, lawyer, or doctor as so many in my family and community hoped I would, I was working to become an artist — a playwright and director. This was (still is) deemed a waste of precious resources and a recipe for failure. Ursula K. Le Guin's novel was a profound confirmation of the value and the necessity of art.

The Dispossessed challenged me to reconsider my worldview and life's choices. In Shevek's stories and struggles, in the non-linear multiple narratives, conflicting ideologies, and philosophical physics, I discovered, or better, recognized myself. The thought-provoking tale of *ambiguous* utopias held out the promise of transformation, renovation, and repair. Here was life and death art! Here was somebody whacking my brain so I could see myself, change the moment I inhabited, and reinvent the world. Here was inspiration and support for who I wanted to be and what I wanted to do — all of which was *the risky unknown*. After finishing *The Dispossessed*, I read every novel that Ursula K. Le Guin wrote, and shared her work with friends, students, colleagues, and even with enemies.

Ursula K. Le Guin writes in the subjunctive case, what might be — a rehearsal of the possible and the impossible. I felt at home in the changeable universe she imagined. After thirty-five years I am still an artist and I now write science fiction and fantasy novels.

Happy Birthday!

ANDREA HAIRSTON
NOVELIST, PLAYWRIGHT/DIRECTOR, PROFESSOR

Will Do Magic for Small Change

ANDREA HAIRSTON

PITTSBURGH, DECEMBER 1984

"Books let dead people talk to us from the grave."

Cinnamon Jones gripped the leather bound, special edition, illustrated adventure book her half-brother Kwame had given her. It was dusty and heavy and smelled of pepper and cilantro. Kwame could never get enough pepper.

"Huh? Don't mutter at me." Opal tugged at the fat tome. "You're too young for that mess! I don't know why Kwame gave it to you. I bet you can't understand half of it."

"How do you know? You haven't read it. Nobody has, except Kwame." Cinnamon talked through gritted teeth and wouldn't let go. She was a big girl, taller than her five-foot-four mother and thirty-five pounds heavier. Opal hadn't won a tug of war with her since she was eight. "I'll be thirteen next August. That's soon."

"What're you mumbling?" Opal said. "Speak up."

"Books let dead people talk to us from the grave!" Cinnamon shouted.

Gasping, Opal let go and Cinnamon tumbled back into the funeral director. "Why did I have such stubborn children?" Opal grimaced. The funeral director nodded at her. He was solemn and upright and smelled like air freshener. Opal had his deepest sympathy and a bill she didn't know how she would pay. Dying was expensive. "Kwame can talk to you at home," Opal whispered to Cinnamon. "You didn't need to bring that stupid book here."

"Kwame said I shouldn't let this book out of my sight." Cinnamon pressed her cheek against the cover. "What if there was a fire at home?"

Opal snorted. "We could collect some insurance."

"This volume's almost a hundred years old. And powerful."

"Kwame picked that old thing up dumpster diving in Shadyside." Opal shook her head. "Dragging trash around with you everywhere won't turn it into magic."

"Why not?"

Opal's voice caught on words that wouldn't come. She shook her head and waved a hand — an *I-can't-take-any-more* gesture. She shuddered and wavered against the flower fortress that surrounded the open casket. Her dark skin had a chalky overlay. The one black dress to her name had turned ash gray in the wash but didn't shrink to fit her wasted form. She was as flimsy as a ghost. Kwame looked more alive than Opal, a half smile stuck on the face nestled in blue satin. Cinnamon scrunched her nose and eyes together. Funerals were stupid. This ghoul statue wasn't really Kwame, just dead dust in a rented pinstripe suit made up to look like him. Kwame was gone.

With gray walls, slate green curtains, olive tight-napped carpets, and the faint tang of formaldehyde clinging to everything, Johnson's Funeral Parlor might as well have been a tomb. In the front parlor, far from the stand-in body, far from the grieving mother and half-sister, mourners in black and navy blue stuffed their mouths with fried chicken or guzzled coffee laced with booze. Uncle Dicky had a flask and claimed he was lifting everybody's spirits. Cinnamon didn't see anybody looking droopy—

mostly good Christians arguing whether Kwame, after such a bad boy life, hit heaven or hell or decayed in the casket.

"God's always busy punishing the wicked," Cousin Raina muttered.

Uncle Dicky nodded. "Indeed He is."

"So Hell must have your name and number, Richard," Aunt Becca said. "This chicken is dry." She munched it anyway and a blob of potato salad. Opal's youngest sister didn't worry about what she put in her mouth or what came out. A hollow tube in a sleek black sheath, Aunt Becca got away with everything. She never took Jesus as her personal savior and nobody made a big stink. Not like when Opal left Kwame's dad for Storm Cooper, a pagan hoodoo man seventeen years her senior. The good Christians never forgave Opal, not even after Cinnamon's dad was shot in the head helping out a couple getting mugged. He and Opal had never married, and now Storm Cooper was in a coma and might as well be dead. This was supposedly God punishing the wicked too. Cousin Raina had to be lying. What kind of god would curse a good man, who risked his life for strangers, with a living death? Cinnamon squeezed the book tighter against her chest. God should make sense.

"I hate these dreary wake things." Funerals even put Aunt Becca in a bad mood. She and her boyfriend steered clear of Kwame's remains.

"The ham's good," the boyfriend said. He was a fancy man, styling a black velvet cowboy shirt and black boots with two inch heels. Silver lightning bolts shot up the shaft of one boot and down one side of the velvet shirt. His big rough rider's hat had feathers and bolts too and edged the other head gear practically off the wardrobe rack. "But why have food with the body?" He helped himself to the mashed sweet potatoes.

"I don't know." Aunt Becca sighed.

Opal couldn't stand having anybody over to their place. It was a dump. Cinnamon kept her mouth shut though. She didn't have to tell everything she knew.

"Some memorial service...nobody saying anything." Aunt Becca looked relieved as she complained.

None of Opal's family loved Kwame the way Cinnamon did. Nobody liked Opal much either, except Aunt Becca. The other uncles, aunts, and cousins came to the memorial service to impress Clarence, Opal's rich lawyer brother, and also to let Opal know what a crappy mom she was. Opal didn't have any friends and Kwame's druggy crew weren't welcome, 'cause they were just "faggots and losers," so boring family was all there was.

"Woman couldn't manage to see Kwame through his seventeenth year," Uncle Clarence whispered loudly to his third wife. Cinnamon forgot her name.

"Mayonnaise is going bad." Aunt Becca made a face at Opal. "Sitting out too long."

"Then don't eat it, Rebecca." Opal shouted over the empty chairs lined up in front of the casket and then looked ready to fall over. "Hell, I didn't make it." She probably needed a cigarette.

"Sorry." Aunt Becca pressed bright red fingernails against plum-colored lips. "You know my mouth runs like a leaky faucet."

Cinnamon leaned against Opal, not enough to knock her over, just enough to offer a little heat. Opal was shivering cold. Cinnamon held her breath and squeezed her eyes shut a second. "This *is* a special book, *magic*; a book to see a person through tough times."

"Kwame talked a lot of crap, you hear me?" Opal touched the stand-in's marble skin and stroked soft wiry hair. "When he was high, he didn't know what he was saying. Just making shit up."

"Don't say that." Cinnamon's lip trembled.

Clarence's grown kids sneered at her foul-mouthed mom. Opal was so embarrassed by a drug-addict son who maybe OD'ed on purpose that she almost didn't have a memorial service. Cursing was fine though. Jehovah's Witnesses like Uncle Dicky, Holy Rollers like Cousin Raina, and other snooty people in the family who didn't believe you should have your mouth in the gutter around children clucked and sucked and shuffled their feet, but held their peace. Opal was the bereaved one after all — they'd have to scold her later.

"Good lord, what size are you already?" Aunt Becca waved a chicken wing at Cinnamon. "You better learn to push yourself away from the table."

"I didn't eat much." Cinnamon didn't eat *anything*. Her belly burned. Sadness always turned her stomach inside out. Tears pounded at her eyes. She sucked most of them back.

"Don't you dare. Nobody wants to see all of that." Opal hated tears. "You promised me not to be a crybaby today! Kwame wouldn't want you crying."

"I knew him better than you did." Kwame wouldn't want Cinnamon to be sad, but he'd appreciate a few tears. "There's all this stuff he didn't tell you."

Opal looked panicked. "Your brother was no good. You hear me?" She gripped Cinnamon's shoulders and stared in her eyes. "That's why he's dead this day." She wheezed and coughed a bit. "I got to get rid of all that stuff of his. Can't have it around the house, bad memories doing us no good..."

"But this book is all true. Can't throw the truth away." Cinnamon stroked the cover. "And the more I read it, the truer it will get! Kwame got it from a weird and wonderful Wanderer, several lifetimes old, ancient, yet young for the Wanderer tribe."

Opal groaned.

"No, wait, see, this Wanderer trusted Kwame to keep several illustrated journals of top, top secrets safe. I don't know where the other volumes are, but… It's a treasure we can't let fall into the wrong hands. A Wanderer from the stars I think, or no, from another dimension, from the spaces between things, chronicling life here on Earth." The floor tilted under Cinnamon's feet. Her tongue tingled. She wasn't telling a normal lie to save herself from a sticky situation or to get what she wanted out of stingy, crazy grown-ups. She wasn't trying to impress folks or make them like her. The Wanderer's story just popped in her mouth. Each delicious word made her feel much better — the natural high Kwame was always jealous of. This lie was good medicine and tasted so sweet, it had to be true. "*A Wanderer from the stars traveling the spaces between things.* That's it. New pages appear every day. Kwame appointed me Guardian of the Wanderer's Earth Chronicles — if anything should happen to him."

"What? Stop it." Opal clutched a throbbing head. "Stop it right now."

Cinnamon couldn't. "He said the Guardian should memorize the Chronicles in case the book is ever destroyed. Kwame was worried that maybe he would let the Wanderer down. He knew he could count on me as backup."

"What did I tell you 'bout lying and making up stuff? You're too old for that."

Cinnamon talked over Opal. "I have to start reading soon or pages will disappear. Kwame said we're about to forget everything. These are trying times." Last week standing in line for a sneak preview of a John Sayles movie, *Brother From Another Planet*, Kwame handed Cinnamon the Chronicles but didn't say much beyond the Guardian bit. Cinnamon often had to fill in the blanks with him. "He said I should read to fortify my soul against Armageddon."

"You don't even know what Armageddon is!" Opal yanked Cinnamon close and pressed chapped lips to her ears. "Kwame was depressed and high all the time, and his baby sister was the only person dumb enough to listen to his crap."

"That's not true. Great Aunt Iris could listen and so could — "

"I don't see anyone from the other side of your family." Uncle Clarence crept up on them, sniffing flowers and eyeing the little sympathy cards. "I know Kwame was no relation of theirs, but…"

"Granddaddy Aidan, Miz Redwood, and Great Aunt Iris are going to be here shortly," Cinnamon lied, "unless they hit further delays. They were supposed to come yesterday, but a freak storm ambushed them up in Massachusetts."

Opal didn't contradict a word, yet Clarence wasn't about to believe Cinnamon's tale. He shook his head and wrinkled his nose, like lies were funky and he smelled a big one. His two grown-up sons sniggered in the corner. Their younger sister did too and she wasn't usually mean. Kwame claimed people got mean in a crowd, even nice people. They couldn't help it — human beings tended to sync up with the prevailing mood. That's why he didn't like to hang with more than four people at a time or hand his mood over to strangers. He and Cinnamon used to practice throwing up shields against mob madness and other bad energy for the times when they might be surrounded by hostiles. Cinnamon tried to raise emergency fortifications, but sagged. Getting her shields up without Kwame was just too hard.

"Miz Redwood is a…a hoodoo conjure woman and she married herself an Indian medicine man." Aunt Becca explained to her boyfriend who was a recent conquest and not up on all the family lore.

"They never got married," Clarence said. "Not in any church."

"Hoodoo?" the boyfriend said over him. "What? Like Voodoo?"

"Old timey *real* black magic," Aunt Becca rubbed Cinnamon's shoulder, "you know?"

He didn't.

"Well, not Hollywood horror, not zombie black folk going buck wild." Aunt Becca shook her head. "They say, old Miz Redwood can still *lay tricks* on folks who cross her." She pursed her lips at Clarence and his grown kids. "Or just jinx anybody she has a mind to. And together, she and Aidan can do all kinds of mischief. Iris got a gentler nature, but nothing gets past her. She can see clear through to your heart."

"Rebecca! Nobody believes that old-timey mess," Opal said. "Lies and backcountry superstition."

Cinnamon winced. Opal was syncing up with the enemy.

"Aidan's over a hundred and Redwood's not far behind! Conjure, roots, spells, and herbs, just keeping 'em going, keeping 'em strong." Aunt Becca nodded at Cinnamon. "That's nothing to sneer at."

"When you get along to my age…" Her boyfriend hesitated. He didn't look old: handsome as sin, a little gray in a droopy mustache but powerful muscles pressing against the velvet shirt. "Well, going on strong is what you want to hear about."

That was two on Cinnamon's side.

"Devil worship and paganism." Uncle Dicky took a swig right from his flask. His hand was shaking. Jitters broke out everywhere in this god-fearing crowd.

"The family thanks you all for coming." The funeral director's voice was a soothing rumble and calmed everybody right down. "Your visiting hour is over in twenty minutes."

"Only twenty? We just got here!" Clarence rolled his eyes. Opal couldn't afford to pay for more memorial time to impress him. Nobody wanted to be here a second longer anyhow. "A budget funeral," Clarence muttered.

"Driving a bus doesn't pay like telling lies in court for guilty people with money to burn." Cinnamon blurted this out fast, before anyone could stop her.

"Where'd she get that from?" Clarence sneered in Opal's face, brushing dandruff from his lapels.

"Cinnamon's a bright child, making up her own mind," Opal replied.

Clarence wanted to hit somebody. Aunt Becca shoved a plate of chicken and gravy soaked biscuits in his hands. "Eat," she said. "Don't nobody want to be carrying this food home."

Opal pulled Cinnamon away. "Why don't you come over here and read your book?" She sat her in a chair by a window onto a vacant lot. "And quit telling tales."

"Words are my shield," Cinnamon said, watching the sun head for the hills and cold fog rise off the river. A homeless man pushed his shopping cart through dead weeds. "I know they're trying hard to get here."

"Your grandparents can't be running down to Pittsburgh for every little thing," Opal whispered. "They're old as the hills. You shouldn't be calling them up and bothering them."

"I didn't call them. They just *know*. They're coming for us. To keep us company, 'cause we're sad."

"You're just making up what you want to happen."

"Granddaddy Aidan, Miz Redwood, and Great Aunt Iris love us. That's enough reason to come. I'm their favorite grandchild."

"You're their only grandchild." Opal turned away, shaking her head, muttering to herself. "How did I get stuck with a stupid optimist?" She sighed. "Read *The Chronicles of the Great Wanderer* and let me have a little peace, all right?"

Cinnamon nodded, relieved that there was no more talk of getting rid of Kwame's book. Opal staggered away. She only had to last twenty more minutes. Aunt Becca's boyfriend put a cup of tea in her hand. Aunt Becca stuck out her jaw, put her hands on her hips, and kept the Holy Rollers *and* the Atheists at bay.

Cinnamon didn't have to worry about her mom. She opened the book. Every time before, fuzzy letters danced across the page and illustrations blurred in and out of focus. If you couldn't stop crying, reading was too hard. But she was the Guardian, with duties and privileges. Everything was clear now. Memorizing the *Chronicles* would fortify her soul. It was a big book — she had to get started. Or else it would take her whole life! ∿

Touch

SHEREE RENÉE THOMAS

MS. CI-CE-LY, that's what she call me. Say it like there's a bunch of zee's in my name. I like the way she do. Make it sound important, like the name come from somewhere you want to be. She call me and I fix her something light to eat. Give her a glass of cool water and sit down next to her, nod my head while she talk. That's all we do. She talk and I listen. Wipe the crumbs from her face, if she let me. She funny about touch, don't like nobody to hardly deal with her. Say she can't stand the feel of other folk flesh against her skin. Don't bother me none, not at all. 'Cause when she talk, I like to listen, but I don't let her know. She say the oddest things, that she do.

Like that first time she tell me her people come from water. Didn't know what she meant by that, so I asked her.

"Come from where?" I say. "What water? You talking 'bout somewhere in Europe?" A lot of these white folk talk about the "old country," even if they ain't never been nowhere near it. Farthest I been is to see my grand-niece in Evanston, but Ms. Rowan shake her head, no. I tell her my people come from Mississippi, maybe that muddy water was what she had in mind. She shake her head again, wave her arms, slow-like, big swooshing motion. "Bigger?" She nod, yes. "Oh," I say. "Your people stay near the ocean." Wrong again. I raise her up, plump the pillow beneath her neck.

Blue lines stretch all 'cross her skin, like water through her veins. "Bigger," I say. "Bigger than the ocean? I don't know no body of water much bigger than that."

And that's when she smile at me, gray eyes sparkling 'til they start to look green. Then I wonder what she looked like before the years started pulling at the skin around her neck and jaws and her eyes. Mine starting to look like that, too, like my body starting to forget itself, like the skin don't remember how to hold onto bone, but I'm my mama's daughter. Be a while 'fore it's full-blown. You know, it ain't true what they say. Black do crack — it just take its time doing it.

I look at Ms. Rowan's head, gray roots leaning back into red, like her ends been touched by the sun, but it's only Miss Clairol. The agency say she sixty-nine, but I know better. She look back at me and smile. Might have been pretty once, way back when. Can't tell now though, 'cause she don't have no pictures in the house, not like natural folk do, not a one. In my time, I have took care of quite a few elders, folk they loved ones remember and some they forget. It get me worried sometime. I don't want to be sitting up in nobody's old folk home, eating Jell-O and unsweetened Kool-Aid, fretting away 'cause I'm lonesome. I may not have no children, but I do have kin. Hoping somebody will be around to look after me, if it do come to that.

But Ms. Rowan don't have nobody. Nobody, unless you count all them statues and knickknacks of bugs she got hanging everywhere. Thangs hanging all over the house, sitting up on her bookshelves and side tables, hanging from expensive, heavy frames on the wall. Water beetles, that's what she call them. No, scarabs. Look like cockroaches to me. She laugh when I say that. Sound like the wind blowing through an old bent tree.

That's Ms. Rowan. She can go days without saying nothing, then when she get started, seem like she never gon' quit.

"As nice a place this is," I tell her, "why you want to be sitting up 'round all these nasty bugs? Don't they scare you?"

"Not bugs," she say, eyes beetling at me like a spider. "Family. And family is where you first learn fear."

She worry me when she start with that oddness. Loving a bug is one thing, calling it your kin is another. And fear in the family. Don't even get me started. Now, I like to collect things, too, much as the next. I like sunflowers, real pretty bright ones, the kind where the petals look like bonnets. I got me some china dishes with sunflowers painted all over them, and my rugs and my towels and things like that got the same sunflower print. I got sunflowers all in my house but can't get none to grow in my yard. But that's alright though. My little shotgun is not as decked out as all this, but if it was, I'd fill it with flowers, not no nasty bugs. Ms. Rowan's got one of those three-stories in midtown, near the park, built back when there wasn't nobody but white folks in North Memphis, them and all they Confederate kin. Statues stashed all over the place like they some kinda Dixie memorial. Now these old houses are bordered up by the 'hood. And there's all kind folk living there would love to have as much room as this to walk through, stretch they legs a bit.

I tell Ms. Rowan this, but she don't listen. Or she do, and keep doing the same, which is nothing. Sitting and staring, laying in that bed, talking nonsense. Scratching her arms, big long scars that don't never seem to heal up, talking 'bout, *where my wings.* You know how old folk do. Set in their ways. This her house, I keep telling myself, and I ain't got to live in it. I have to tell myself this every time I mess around and stumble on one of them bugs she like to caress, holding and stroking them, calling them out by name like they kin and friend. Just come through three days out of seven, dust up some, shake a few pans and some sheets, cook her up a mess of meals and listen to her talk about her *family*. She mad about them bugs, convinced they as good as people, love them more than anybody out in the street. Ain't never heard her say different.

What kind of mess is this?

The other day she asked me to get her uncle from the top shelf.

"Your uncle? Ms. Rowan, I ain't got time for this today. I got laundry to do, and you claim you want some hot cakes — from scratch. Hot cakes for lunch, hot as it is, and I ain't never heard of such…"

"I'm getting so dry," she say. "I need water…"

I look at her real close. Do seem like her skin kind of parched. Them scars kind of scab up. Her lips chapped a bit, something awful really, like she ain't had a drop of water in days. And if she had have been a sister, she would have been ashy, would have needed a whole pot of Vaseline to fix her up, but she all splotchy splotchy — you know how some of them get — look like she bout to peel off and hit the floor.

She keep grumbling and I shake my head. She don't look so good.

"Ocean?" I say, frowning. "I can't hardly tell where you from with that accent. What you gon' do with the ocean? Too much salt in it, you can't drink it. 'sides, I just bought you three glasses of water. How much water can a soul drink?"

She smile then, real funny like she remember an old joke.

"Don't drink water," she say. "Breathe it. Give me another glass, Cicely. I can't feel my wings."

"Ms. Rowan, you ain't gon' worry me today," but I put the linen down and go get her glass. She drink it greedily, hands trembling, eyes closed so tight would have thought she just dragged up out the desert. I let her hold on to the tumbler and consider giving her the pitcher. *No, don't nobody need that much water, I don't care how thirsty they is.* I wipe the yellow counter down, careful not to knock one of her knickknacks on the floor. These bugs sho' starting to worry me. Look like she got more stashed around the house than the last time I was here. I pick up one, wrinkling my nose. It don't smell bad, just a faint hint of alcohol or something, and it's shiny, like it's been covered in varnish. Its blue body sparkles and gleams in the afternoon sun peeking through the kitchen window. The other one is a dark green, with bits of orange and a big ole mouth shaped like a can opener. Why she want these thangs sitting up in her kitchen, of all places, I'll never know. That's why she ain't got no company.

She can't stand for me to talk too bad about them, get all hincty. The first time the agency sent me over and I tried to throw some of the real ugly, dusty ones out, she liked to have a fit. "Leave them be," she say, eyes so narrow and squinty I thought they had sunk right back in her head. "And I never call you out your name, so you'd do well not to bad-talk my people." *Her people?* Child please! If my niece hadn't messed around and got herself another baby, I would've been told the agency they could kiss my natural ass. Between this and my other overnight jobs they got me rotating, I can just barely keep my house payments up and send a little extra to Laqueshia and 'nem in Illinois. She keep talking 'bout she gon' visit, but I know she just talking. I might have to take some leave and go on up there to see about her and that baby.

·

They came and took Ms. Rowan last night. Got her 'round midnight. Neighbors say they took her from her bed and didn't even change her nightclothes. Just dragged her to the ambulance and dumped her at the Home. When I got to her house the next morning, she was gone, and it don't look like she took any of her bugs with her.

It took me a while to work my nerves up enough to go see her. Last time I was in a home like that, it was to see my own grandmama, and the way she looked at me when I left her there made me never want to come back again. Don't seem right to live your life right, only to end up holed up in one of them old folk farms, put out to pasture. Ms. Rowan had more grit than anybody I know, but I couldn't rightly tell how she might make out in a state home.

When I went to see her, the child at the front desk made me wait outside for forty minutes. Sound like she wasn't doing nothing but talking to her boyfriend or somebody, but when I ask her what's the trouble, she start shuffling paper like she busy. And when I finally did get to Ms. Rowan's room, it took me a minute to catch my breath. They had her dressed in work overalls, with her room and bed number stenciled on the front, name of the unit on the back. *Getwell Gardens*, please. One of those trapdoors low on the bottom, I guess for easy access. When I come to the bed, she wouldn't even speak to me. Look like her gray eyes carry blame, they so dark they flint. But how was I supposed to know they'd take her so quickly? Thought I was slick coming through there, tidying up like I always did, fixing her food, and listening, always listening to her water tales of bug life, even after the agency sent that last warning. How was I supposed to know they'd get through her paperwork so quickly? As many cases they got, seem like it would have took longer 'fore they realized that my assignment was long overdue. But they run the Homes like they do everything else in this city. If you can't pay, can't nobody but God help you. Budget crisis got them cutting every corner. No room in the inn, they just pat you down and sign you off into the ward.

Don't nobody leave.

Break my heart. I don't want my last days spent in no dirty diapers and oversized overhauls, in a cold, unfamiliar room, touched by strangers.

"Ms. Rowan?"

She don't answer at first. Just laying in that little hard bed, the pillow so flat she probably got a crook in her neck. I put my bag down and pull a chair to her bedside.

"Ms. Rowan, it's me. Cicely." Her eyes are closed, but I see her lids flicker a bit. The skin so thin and dry, it sounds like the pages of a book turning. "What they got you in here doing? Breaking the law? Up to no good?" I try to get her to laugh, but she won't acknowledge me, so I sit still a minute, letting my eyes take in this piece of a room.

She had one window with no view. It looked over the roof of the complex, and from what I could tell, look like a new group of inmates were coming in a van. Could have been a death car, far as they were concerned, 'cause I could tell from the plastic flowers, the shabby chair, and the lumpy rug centered in the room, they didn't expect much company here and made no effort to sweeten these folk's lives. All I could do was shake my head and try to sound cheerful.

"Ms. Rowan, I brought you something."

Her eyelids flickered a bit, trembling like thin paper. "I don't know what they been feeding you in here, and finicky as you is, I 'spect you ain't eating no matter what it is. But fix your lips for this!" I waved a big slice of potato pie before her, hoping she'd stop playing sleep and rise up a bit.

"Come on, Ms. Rowan, you know I don't be playing with my sweet potato pie. Not everybody get this gift I'm laying on you."

Then I hear it, sound like a dry husk, cicada skin in the wind. "Ci-ce-ly," she say, like her chords rusted in her throat, her lips so chapped, she don't say *water* she say it like this, *"wata."* I hold the pie a moment, feeling stupid, then wrap it back up in the aluminum foil, place it on the side table. "Ms. Rowan, what they don' done to you?"

She straining a moment, chest heaving slow, her face pained, then I see why. There's just enough light in the room for me to see the slow tear ease down the wrinkles in her face, her skin so dry, don't even look like she got enough *wata* in her to make no tears.

Lord, why did I think some pie was gon' cheer her up?

After my eyes don' took in nearly every inch of the room, the tow-down faded curtains, the mismatch furniture, and the empty Tupperware pitcher, I scoot my chair closer to her, forcing myself to really see her.

Now, I could be wrong, but I don't believe Ms. Rowan wasn't never no beauty queen, still she had an order about her that made you respect what God give her all the same. But it's clear from the dry patches on her jaw and chin that she ain't been herself since she come here. Ms. Rowan hair all disheveled like it ain't been touched in ages. I dig in my purse to see if I brought a comb. I push aside an old pay stub, come up with a nail clipper and a few sticks of Big Red, but no comb. I put the bobby pins on the side table and see what I can do with my fingers, cramped as they is.

Ms. Rowan don't move away when I reach for her, so I know she feeling bad. Her hair feels thin, lifeless. There ain't but a touch of Clairol left, faded crimson on her brittle ends. Her scalp all scabby, like all her hair 'bout to fall out, and I brush away little flakes that disappear in my hand. She smell funny, too, but not like that Ajax and lemons the Home use to keep the piss smell from drifting in the hall, not musk or sweat either, but an iron scent, copper like blood or some strange metal, something I ain't never smelled before.

"When the last time they wash yo' hair?" I say and laugh to keep from crying. Her eyelids flicker but she don't answer. She turn her head a little, closer to me. *That's better*, I think. "Somebody got to clip your ends. Wish I'd thought to bring my comb," I say as I struggle with a knot, parting the hair with my fingers and twisting her stringy strands into a cornrow, tight like the way my grandmama used to do me.

Ms. Rowan lay there, still as silence. I sing a hymn while I twist an end, then gently lay the braid over her shoulder. "Now that's pretty," I say, pleased, though the part's not as straight as it could be. Just when I'm thinking I'd better leave, her hands clamp my wrist.

"Cicely," she say, holding my wrist so tight. I want to pull away. "I come from the *wata*, the *wata* is the cradle, the *wata* is my birth. My people come from the *wata*, ancient breed of life. I come from the river, the one you call Mississippi, but I ain't the last, just the last 'round here. My people the first life, the first that come on the planet. For us, all *wata*, all bugs is sacred. The *wata* hold us, the lifeforce of this planet. Though most fear, I am not, we are not your enemy."

She squeezing me, talking so fast, that iron scent all around me.

"I have lived millennia," she say, rising up, her pointy elbow digging in her bed sheet, "never far from the *wata*, never far from the source. But Cicely, this body growing weak. I need *wata*."

I don't know what to make of all that. Sound like she don' lost all her natural mind. But even crazy folk deserve they dignity, it don't make no sense to have nobody living like this.

"Ms. Rowan, don't you got no people I can call?"

She look at me, her face all slack, eyes narrowing, like I'm the dumbest child in the room. She look at me like I ain't heard a word she said, she look at me and say *"wata!"* then point to the bathroom.

She struggling to get up, so I push back my chair, return to home aide mode. This is what I know how to do. I let her lean against me as she trembles, trying to stand, that's when I see her feet. The poor thing's nails ain't been clipped, her heels are ashy, and I didn't have but a sample size of shea butter when she need a whole pot of grease.

"Steady now," I say, but she feel like air in my hands. Her bones so thin, I wouldn't be surprised if I could see Adam's rib. We take our time getting 'cross the floor, and she holding on me tight, raspy breathing in my ear. Not breathing, humming, hymnlike, *"wata, wata,"* over and over again, like a prayer.

When I peel her overalls off, I nearly drop her. Her body is covered in this thick, clear squooshy stuff, like baby oil gel, but it smell like iron, and it take all I got not to just put her in the tub and leave. Let them Home folk deal with it, but that ain't my nature, and the City don't care no way.

I sit her in the tub, in that stall that look like a big high chair, take a sponge and the little bit of hard black soap that's more like brine. I wash her back, gentle as I can, but when the sponge come up, I see it's covered in a layer of skin. I search, but she not bleeding nowhere, steady humming, like it feel good. I don't know how long I keep this up before I get her all cleaned. The water look funny, yellow at first, then kinda sparkly, then I wrap her in a towel, dry off her, and lead her back to the chair. Her eyes seem brighter now, she watching me as I strip the stained sheets from her bed. I pull a clean set from a dresser, make up her bed, carry her in my arms, she holding tight like she carrying me.

"You need anything?" I ask, reaching for my purse. I flick a ladybug from my wrist and hoist the bag over my shoulder. "I'll be back, maybe early next week."

She look at me hard, like she know the truth ain't in me, but don't say nothing, just lay there, playing sleep.

I am almost out the door, when her steady voice stop me.

"Cicely," she say, "do this for me..."

Can't believe I'm out here digging in the garbage.

Work all my life, sometime two, three jobs, since I was seventeen, and here I am, *still* a bag lady. Ms. Rowan better be glad I call myself a Christian, even though I don't show up at church but twice a year. Better be glad, 'cause had it been for anybody else, them thangs would've still been sitting in the street.

I come to the house early this morning, thinking I'd get here before anybody I know see me, but don't you know the City don' already throwed all her stuff out, got it sitting up in black garbage bags on the curb. I would've knocked on the door, just to see who they got up in there now, but I wanted to get this mess and be gone so I can get back home and fix me something to eat before my next shift.

Now I wasn't in the door good, before that little girl at the front desk stop me.

"You've come to see 3WRWP60?" she say, staring at me like I stole something.

"What?"

"The client on the third floor, in Permanent Housing?"

"Ms. Rowan? Yes, I'm Ms. Harris, I come to see 'bout her. Why?" She purse her lip and speak real slow, like I'm three years old. "Well, Ms. Harris, we wondered if you could speak with her. There have been," she paused, "problems."

"What kinda problems?" I ask, suspicious. They better not start nothing up in here, because I can't do nothing with Ms. Rowan. I stare at the girl's pass key, see her name is Aminata.

"After you left, we found her wandering in the grounds."

I take this in, trying to figure out how Ms. Rowan get the strength to walk anywhere, as bad a shape she in. How you lose some old folk, anyway? But it's clear these folk in the Home don't pay nobody no attention.

"Well, how she get there?"

The girl don't answer. Keep talking like she ain't just heard me speak. "Ms. Harris, if she keeps breaking curfew, we will have to reassign her." She stares at me, and I know what that means.

"Is that all?" I ask. This ain't a train of thought I want to follow.

She stop, like she trying to think of what *not* to say. "There is just one thing."

"Yeah?"

"She refuses to eat. The aides say she has refused all of her meals for a whole week."

She motions for an aide, and he brings me a tray. I take a look under the cover and sigh, don't look like nothing a starving man would want to eat. I hug my purse close to me and balance the tray as the aide opens the door.

"You know, ma'am, she don't give us no trouble," he says, loud whispering like he ain't used to being heard. His gray uniform is neat, and I see somebody taught him to press his slacks, polish his shoes. Nice young man, look like he got home training. "She just keep getting up and walking. They mad 'cause don't nobody know how she get out, she got the run of the place. When we found her, she was standing in the fountain, fully dressed." He give me a look like he want to say more, then as he close the door, "My grandmama stayed here, too."

I thank him, not sure what to say to that and like to drop the tray when I come through. Ms. Rowan sitting up in that bed, damn near blacker than me. If I didn't know better I would have thought that she'd been down in Miami sunbathing.

"Well, where *you* been?" I ask, putting the tray down, hoping I can get her to laugh. But when I sit down beside her, the joke catch in my throat. It ain't just that her skin don' tanned, practically like we could be kin, but it's all scaly, like there's a thin web just under the skin. I try not to let the shock take over my face, but it's hard.

"Ms. Rowan, you ain't looking like yourself."

She wait a minute, throw her head way back and holler, the laughter womb deep.

"Cicely," she say, her voice so low. I got to lean in close to make my ear reach.

She wipe a tear from her eye, say, "You ain't stopping no men in the street either."

Dang if she ain't still salty. I plop my purse on the table and dig around, like I'm mad. "Here," I say and hand her the green glass beetle. It's the only one in all the bags that wasn't smashed up or half broken, and now I'm ready to leave.

"Look, I don't know what you been doing, but whatever it is, you need to stop. These folk don't play with you here. If the Home transfer you to Mental, there ain't nothing else I can do. Ain't no visitors there and well, truth is," I say, looking down, "I don't rightly know what else I *can* do."

I look back up, but she ain't paying me no mind. She holding that dang beetle, her *kinfolk*, like it is the Hope diamond.

"Ms. Rowan," I say, but her fingers working, stroking its glossy green back, its long wings. I stand up and zip my bag and try not to grieve. "I'll be back," I say, "but maybe not next week. I'll be back, okay?"

She don't say nothing when I leave.

The next time I come she gone.

A white-haired man, turned on his side, snoring like grizzlies. I guess that's his family over there, trying to convince themselves to hang around 'til he wake up and not slink out like thieves.

"And that ain't my daddy," his son say, crying, the woman at his side, making calm-down motions, rubbing the small of his back like he the baby. "The lips, the eyes, the shape of his head, the cheeks don't favor him."

I stand in the doorway, turning to leave when the baby, cutest thang, dressed in a blue jumpsuit, tear away from his father's grasp. "Ooh, bub!" he cries as he run to stand before the window.

Ladybugs, hundreds of them, orange and red with speckled backs covered the glass, a bright, wavering ribbon.

The water is cold.

"Mama Cece?"

Sound like somebody calling my name from far away. I open my eyes and find my fingers and toes all wrinkly.

"How long I been sitting in this tub, child?"

Laqueshia shrug her shoulders, "I dunno," she say and hand me my robe.

"Where Buba at?"

"We going to the backyard."

"Alright, I'll see you there."

I put my house dress on and head out back. I can hear Buba squealing before the screen door shut.

"Whatchu doing out here?" I say before I see the other child.

She standing in my yard, near my sunflowers, Buba pulling up weeds, laughing and giggling at her feet.

"Where you come from, child?" I ask. Laqueshia just shake her head. The girl is a long-legged, redheaded thing, no more than four or five, with gray eyes glimmering so, in the fading light they almost look green.

She holds a wild dandelion, blows, the seedlings fly off in the breeze. Up, up, and up again. She smiles at me, waiting. Her skin is luminous and smooth, clear as water.

"Ms. Rowan?" I say, bending so low, I feel the ache pull at my knees.

The sun is fading fast. Mosquito buzz, gnat whine fill the darkening air. A breeze kicks up from the east, and grandmama's willow tree seems to lean in close to listen. The child looks at me, her mouth full of bees, zees, recognition in her eyes, says "Ci-ce-ly."

She raises tiny clenched fists and stares expectantly.

Unsure, I point to the right. She shakes her head no, impish grin.

I point to the left, Buba giggles, crawling to her mama on little square knees.

The red child don't speak, but thrusts her open palm at me. An emerald beetle with long silvery wings rests in the palm of her unlined hand.

"Touch," she say and smiles at me.

Lightning bug reflects a mason jar of silence, there's gold dust in my hand. ～

~: I MUST HAVE BEEN about five, because I know I couldn't tie my shoes yet, and we were still living in my dad's friend Jim's house. I remember the smell of rice cooking, the sun in the window over the kitchen sink, my mother's back to me as she stood washing something.

I had come from my room with a puzzle, a very specific question that I was unable to fully articulate. "Mom, why am I here?"

"Why are you here in the kitchen?" My mother asked, glancing over her shoulder, amusement stirring in her voice. That was not what I meant.

"No." I stamped my foot, shoelaces flopping on the linoleum. "Why am I…" I studied the dark brown of my upper arm, poked at the very solid flesh and looked up at her, at a loss… "here?"

"Oh," she said. There was another pause and the sound of the stove clicking off.

"You are here," Mom said, "to FIND OUT why you're here." She made it sound like a grand adventure, like a story that would continue to unfold. She made it OK not to know; made the process of discovery a gift.

When I was twelve, my mother gave me a copy of *The Lathe of Heaven*. Mom's antidote to 1970s suburban mall culture and rising pre-adolescent tension was fantasy and science fiction. *The Lathe of Heaven* was the first (but definitely not the last) of Ursula K. Le Guin's books that we read. In it, the Aliens call George Orr's reality-changing dreams *iahklu'*. The Aliens, themselves manifested out of Orr's dreaming, have a greater understanding of the process than Orr or the self-appointed expert Dr. Haber, yet are unable to fully explain it. They understand that calling forth reality is a responsibility to be shared, and teach Orr what to say to summon assistance: *Er' perrehnne*. Mom and I talked about George Orr like he was family and about the things we would dream (President

Chisholm!). We cheered Heather Lelache's brown-skinned biracial presence as much as her profession and practical mind. On second read, we decided that *iahklu'* must be a kind of spiritual practice, like meditating while you're asleep, and you get to connect with the whole universe while you do it. We talked more about reality (not as certain as one might think) and community (necessary. At some point, everybody needs a little help from their friends).

Ms. Le Guin, your work remains part of my "finding out" process, inspiring wonder and affirming infinite possibility and the essentiality of imagination and community. Happy Birthday and many more, always.

AMA PATTERSON

Seamonsters

AMA PATTERSON

I

"DAMN. Ain't she *never* gon' drop that baby?" Shirl's voice drips into the thick, midafternoon air and pops like spit in a hot greased skillet. Makes me wanna jump back 'fore I get burned. It's too hot to be startin' shit. It's too hot to be sitting on this red plastic couch Miz Lucy got on the porch; gotta put a towel under your butt to keep from sticking to the seat. I don't know how Shirl can stand it with them braces on her legs. Twelve-and-a-half pounds of metal and leather just so she can stand between two crutches, when she ain't in that wheelchair. Heat lingers, fingers bags of BonTon chips and boiled peanuts, sets a spell on a crate of Orange Nehi, makes conversation with a few flies humming lazily in and out. Heat, like me 'n Shirl, just be passing the time. Even the hands on the wall clock are droopin' in the heat, tho' that clock ain't kept time since time began. Even in the shade of the porch at Miz Lucy's, with that clackety black metal fan slapping at the heat from up on top of the Frigidaire, and the front and back doors of the store propped wide, it's damn near too hot to turn my head. Air full of salt, and not the slightest hint of a breeze. I turn anyway, and see VidaMae making her usual slow, waddling progress down Marsh Road. VidaMae turning the corner puts you in mind of a big diesel truck trying to twist itself down these little streets between the highway and the docks. Sweat makin' her face shine like chrome, and the rest of her is all hip fenders, butt bumpers and a big ol' payload — 'cept hers is in the front.

" 'Oman been pregnant long as there's been dirt." Shirl toss her head, whippin' them long, Indian straight pigtails 'round her shoulders. "Least since…since after…" she kinda crunches up her face, and her voice trails off. Shirl do have a tendency to sort of drift out on you sometimes. I give her a minute to let it pass. "How many kids she got?"

"None livin'," I say, resisting the urge to remind Shirl that she knows this already. I get up to see if Glory and Honor done drank all the lemonade, or if there might yet remain a trickle for another mouth. Them two boys are a plague of locusts in any kitchen, and a pain in the ass on any given day, but they sweet and they mine. "This be her firstborn," I say.

"Hmmph," is all Shirl say, which is a powerful improvement over her usual: a slew of conjecture with a double helping of condemnation. Who does VidaMae think she is, anyway, walkin' to an' fro everyday, and what's she doin? Ain't swimmin', fishin', or meetin' no boat, but there she goes without so much as a good afternoon for anybody, not that anybody in their right mind gon' speak back 'cos something 'bout VidaMae just ain't right. And so on. And on. The more Shirl talks, the more riled up she gets. Her big hands are hard and knuckly from grippin' those crutches or bumpin' that wheelchair over these cart tracks we got for roads; look like crab claws and she wavin' 'em in my face.

Shirl's my sister, so I gotta love her, but she stays confused and her tongue got more barbs than a sticker bush. Heartbreak don't have to make a body hateful.

There's no lemonade to be had. I know Miz Lucy wouldn't mind if I helped myself to an RC or somethin' but I got a taste for lemonade. Shirl still runnin' her mouth. I say a quick prayer for VidaMae and her babies, and for me an' mine, 'cos if some syrup and lemons don't walk themselves up in here before Shirl gets done ranting, it really *will* get hot.

II

VidaMae shuts and double-locks the door of her small apartment, drops her heavy backpack, breathes in dust and quiet, tips silently past drawn shades and covered mirrors. Once she liked her rooms open, sunlit and shining but glass surfaces are a source of terror these days. She knows she just walked in from the concrete, asphalt, and steel of the city, but beyond her windows green trees border on a narrow dirt road. Instead of her own reflection, a strange woman, light-skinned with a face as lean as a blade, stares mockingly through her mirrors, hissing tempting insults. All in all, it is easier not to look. Her bedroom is all in green, a cool glade of pine, ivy, and mint, shaded by fern sheers.

There is a chitinous tapping within the floorboards. Or maybe it's just the building settling, releasing the day's heat.

Mama? It's Tyco. Tyco, he's a good boy. Good to his mama, in spite of everything.

We home now, Mama. Take off your shoes. Gratefully, VidaMae toes her scuffed sneakers off her swollen feet. Pretty soon, all she'll be able to wear is her house shoes. That's better, but not good enough. VidaMae stands, undoes the drawstring on her pants, and shrugs off the blouse, long and generously cut, that conceals her belly. Both garments settle around her ankles in an indigo puddle. VidaMae steps out of it in relief, stretching her arms above her head, lifting her heavy braids off her perspiring neck. She looks past her belly to the floor and squats to retrieve a white business card from the spill of fabric. The card is bent at the corners from much handling and heavy with the weight of impending decisions. VidaMae has been carrying it around for what feels like forever.

Oakcrest Clinic, PA
Abortion Services to 20 weeks
Reasonable fees. Sedation available.
Pregnancy Testing. Birth Control. Individual Decision Counseling.
Appointments Monday–Saturday

VidaMae flips the card over, scans the address she has already memorized: 7 Marsh Road, Waterside....

VidaMae blinks. Reads again, slowly: 1212 East 68th Street, Suite 70...

The lime-green muslin covering her dresser mirror ripples sinuously, like a water snake crossing a still pond. VidaMae freezes, waiting for the mirror woman to start hissing in her ear.

Okay, now get you something to eat. Tyco breaks the tension.

"...lemonade..." Kaycie's cravings nudge VidaMae from the inside like tiny fists. VidaMae licks her lips, tasting tart, cold sweetness.

The green muslin slaps the mirror glass.

Mama. Mama!

Her baby boy. VidaMae sighs. "Yes, Precious?"

Mama, did you see, in the water?

"See what, baby?"

Me! I'm in the water, Mama. I go like this. Sound of babybubbles kissing the air, breathy little pops. A pause. Precious laughs mischief and malice. *Come down to the water, mama.* Splash of needy greedy fat little arms open wide. *Maaamaaa...*

You betta shut up, warns Ty. *Always talkin' some mess. Kaycie?*

Silence.

Kaycie!

Shhh, said VidaMae, finally, patting her belly. She just don't feel like talkin'.

She gon' be like Shirl, Precious sing-songs. *Shirl never talks to you.*

There is a long, green silence.

Well. You can't blame her, says Tyco, finally. It is worse than any casual cruelty. VidaMae closes her eyes.

From Precious, a bubbling, watery laugh: *You gon' make Kaycie swim, Mama? She'll be good at it. It runs in the family… Bet you can swim, Mama. Can't you…?*

Shut up! Tyco snaps.

MAKE ME!

The boys plunge away, leaving the dust to settle into silence once more.

Lemonade forgotten, VidaMae lies down on top of the ivy patterned coverlet, on her left side, just like at that other clinic that first time: marooned on a narrow cot, pierced and deflated, leaking seawater while the nurse searched the waiting room, found no one waiting for VidaMae, and finally sent her home in a cab with prescriptions and meaningless advice.

"I wasn't ready," she reminds them all, "to be nobody's momma." VidaMae hugs her eternally swollen belly.

"…ready now…?" Kaycie twists within her mother's embrace.

But VidaMae is already asleep.

III

Near dark, Miz Lucy's back from wherever it is she goes, and Shirl's gone down to The Bucket, where she sings most nights while Moss Robinson or Ben Rayburn's son James picks the box. Singing is the only thing that seems to smooth ol' Shirl out. I 'spect she got that voice to balance out her nature. Even sticker bushes gotta bloom sometime.

It's been too hot to even think about cooking. I sent Glory and Honor off to Briscoe's for fried fish sandwiches, and gave them extra for ice cream, since they had pooled their bait money and brought me back lemons and syrup. A mite later than I'd wanted it, but right on time, nonetheless. Sweet boys, like I said.

"How were things," asks Miz Lucy, like she's expecting to hear something new and different. She heads straight for the Frigidaire, though there's not a drop of sweat on her narrow, high-yellow face. I shrug.

"Mister Mimms came 'round for his BC powders and Ballantine."

"You could set a clock by that man's hangovers," say Miz Lucy, prying the cap off her own bottle of cold beer.

"Janecee's kids came in for breakfast again. Little Debbies and Seven-Up. She owes you a nickel."

Miz Lucy chuckles and smothers a burp. "Hate to be their mama. Love to be their dentist."

"Corliss picked up for the Bolito Man. 397 straight and combination? What you dream last night?"

"Fish." Miz Lucy spreads her own towel and settles herself on the red plastic couch. "Dead baby fish, swimmin' all 'round the ocean."

That ain't in your dreambook, I think. That ain't even your dream.

Out loud, I say: "And of course, ol' Shirl sat up here 'most all day." 'Oman could talk the ears off a brass monkey.

"Don't I know it." Miz Lucy lights one of her nasty cigarettes, huffing out the match in a thick grey cloud. Nobody else's Lucky Strikes smell like bad eggs. I cough, move to the far end of the couch. "Who she bad-mouthin' today?"

"Who else? Wish she'd just let it be."

"Don't know why she should," say Miz Lucy. "'Oman yank *you* out by the roots and throw you away, you might have a different feeling on the matter."

"Shirl don't know 'bout all that," I say.

"She don't remember, but she do know."

I roll my eyes. "'Zat why she so spiteful?"

"I 'spect so," say Miz Lucy matter-of-factly, draining the last of her beer. Much as I hate to admit it, Miz Lucy's right. I don't wanna end up like Shirl.

"You might not," say Miz Lucy, as if I'd spoken aloud. I hate when she does that.

"But you don't know that fo' sure," I say. This is not a question.

Miz Lucy look sharp at me. "So you rit t' make a deal?" I study the warp of the boards in the porch floor, say nothing. Miz Lucy blow another stank puff in my direction. "We all get what we settle for, Kaycie. You just took matters into your own hands. Can't say as I blame you. Where would you be if you hadn't? All at sea, that's where. All y'all." Miz Lucy chuckles at her own joke, but it ain't nothin' funny. *Taking* a place, a place to be, a place you can't get tore out of is one thing, but *keeping* it is another.

I think about never seeing Glory and Honor come whooping 'round that bend in the road with a string of porgies, never hearing them laughing together at night when they 'sposed t' be 'sleep. There's compensations for the extra washing and the empty icebox. I think about wiggling through briny, blood-dark depths, crippled, discarded and disowned, washing out on the flats at low tide, mad and mean like Precious or half-crazy like Shirl. I shiver, despite the heat, and try *not* to think about that conch shell Mister Briscoe found tangled in his fishing nets and let me keep. I got it buried in the dirt beneath Miz Lucy's porch with seven new pennies. Safe. For right now, anyhow.

Miz Lucy still staring at me. "So do we have a deal?"

I shrug.

"Mind the store for me again tomorrow?"

"Okay." Why not? I'm just waiting. Holding on as long as I can 'tween Miz Lucy and VidaMae. As they say, 'tween the devil and the deep blue sea.

IV

VidaMae, seeking forests, dreams oceans instead: dark, craggy caverns and grottoes beneath the tides. She tugs frantically at urchins and anemones anchored to moss-colored walls; she has to pull them out or else the cave will be filled with grasping fronds. They are stubborn and hard to uproot. The harder she pulls, the more firmly they attach, and once they bloom, it's forever. She struggles as the floating tendrils caress her insistently, wrap themselves lovingly around her waist, tighten around her throat, insinuate themselves between her legs, and sprout deep within her. Panicked, VidaMae flails out and up, up, up…

The air is harder to breathe than the water, and her legs ache beneath her weight. Lights, visible between the trees, illuminate painted wooden signs:

THE BUCKET. COLD BEER. MUSIC. OPEN EVERY NIGHT.
COME ON INN.

VidaMae drifts toward them like a moth.

The Bucket sits on a curving dead-end dirt track about half way between Miz Lucy's and the bluffs, a tiny shack with two tarp walls and a big, wrap-around porch. The bar, a small stage and a few tiny tables are inside, but the real spot is the porch. The front porch is where folks stand, drink, tap their feet to the music, or dance when the beat gets good. The back porch is where you take your business if you got no business doing it. A big, old oak leans over the back rail, dropping acorns like good gossip and begging for an excuse to fall.

VidaMae stands among the trees, invisible to the anonymous souls out back. The evening air is full of cigarette smoke, the clink of beer bottles, scraps of conversation, laughter, and the occasional angry shout. And Shirl. Her Shirl. It is the first time VidaMae has heard her sing.

Somebody's working that slide guitar, urged on by handclaps and hollers. Shirl's voice swoops up, rasping at the crest, a burr caught under an angel's wing.

> ...*Got no one to love me, no one caaares if I live or die*
> *Won'tcha take me hoomme Momma, if I go dowwwwn*
>   *to the water side...*

I love you, thinks VidaMae, but the laughter from the porch sounds like derision. Shirl's voice is as insistent as a pointing finger. Forests, thinks VidaMae, desperately. Oaks like old sistahs; dark, sheltering arms wrapped in shawls of pale moss. Support. Refuge. She finds the marsh instead, the road, the porch, the voices receding to a border of solemn, stately trees, then a sea of tall, golden reeds parted by the inlet. The ribbon of black water reflects the silver moonlight. Bullfrogs singing to whip-poorwills herald the night. VidaMae inhales the fragrance: pine and sweet honeysuckle; the tang of salt.

A splash. Something broods just visible beneath the waterline. The reeds rustle.

Mama? Tyco sounds happy and surprised. *Mama!* VidaMae turns. Tyco is stretched full length on his belly, propped up on his elbows, just his head and shoulders visible between the parted reeds like he'd crawled there playing soldier, smiling up at her, the day's mud and sunshine smudging his cheeks and forehead. VidaMae wants to kiss him and brush the twigs from his hair, wants to hold him to her and — something. Tell him a story? She can't tell. His face is hard to fix on — like a baby one minute, and a grown man the next, like grandmas always say kids do.

"You alright, baby?"

I'm glad to see you. Tyco ducks his head like he's shy. *You don't never come down to see us.*

'Cos you're always with me, thinks VidaMae, but doesn't know how to make it not sound mean. Her oldest, her big boy, always kind and loving. She sits beside him in the gritty mud and slips her hand in his. Wouldn't hurt him for the world. Or so she'd thought.

At the time, she'd thought she was doing right by all of 'em.

Unbidden, Shirl's tune slips past her lips. She lets it. Don't mamas sing to their children?

I know that song, says Tyco, laying his head on her knee. *Don't know the words, though.* His soiled shirt rides up above where brown boy skin gives way to rough, dark, rectangular scales. He wriggles, and there is a swishing in the reeds too far away for boy feet. VidaMae looks, but can only bring herself to touch his hands, his hair.

"Y'all come down here to play?" An honest question, for all that VidaMae does want to change the subject.

Sometimes. Well, not Shirl. But me and Precious, most times we stay in the water. VidaMae looks questioningly at the marsh, the inlet, the black ribbon eddying under the silver light.

"This water right here?"

Tyco's small hand lingers shyly on VidaMae's belly. *Water,* he says. His other hand makes an expansive gesture, the seas of the world in the curve of his palm. He laughs delightedly at the restless movements beneath VidaMae's belly skin.

"…ask her…"

Hi, Kaycie.

"…ask…"

Tyco sighs. His hand pats VidaMae's stomach, keeps his eyes there. *Mama, what you gon' do about Kaycie?*

What you THINK she gon' do? VidaMae jumps at the familiar, bitter sing-song, but too late to avoid the teeth tearing at the tender flesh of her ankle. VidaMae screams, crawls, stumbles away from the pain, from Precious' savage laugh, from Tyco's sad *"Bye, Mama,"* running blind, blunders through haints and shades, trips over knotty roots. Snakes dip from low branches, hissing like the mirror woman. VidaMae lands, sprawling, in a circle of trees. She hugs the earth and sobs with relief. The sistah oaks bend to inspect her, rustling their mossy shawls, murmuring *shhh* and *here nah*, their ruffled heads inclining gracefully toward one another as they confer.

Cousin, one says gently, *this not your place.*

VidaMae wakes gasping. The clinic card is crumpled in her left fist. Her ivy bed smells of the sea.

v

"Where them two rag-muffin children of yours," Shirl fumes into another morning of heat and salt funk. Her legs stick straight out in them braces, taking up the whole red plastic couch — not that I mind.

"They 'round," I say, keeping words to a minimum. This morning I got 'em up early, fed 'em corncakes and molasses, and allowed as to how since I'd be minding Miz Lucy's again, this would likely be a good day to go help Mister Briscoe with his nets. Ain't seen 'em since their plates were licked clean. Times when I'm tempted to judge them solely on legs and appetite, they do show a glimmering of common sense. More than I got, sometimes, 'cos after all, where am I?

I'm hoping Shirl ain't on her usual evil stick, 'cos today just ain't the day. Woke up this morning feelin' wrung out, like I'd spent all night fighting a battle that weren't mine no how. There's a low cloud malingering over Waterside, holding the heat tight. Miz Lucy done give me the keys to the store, which ain't been locked up in a month 'a Sundays, and when I asked her why, she just smile sideways and slide on off 'bout her business. Look more like a snake every day. I stashed two pitchers of lemonade in the fridge, though. I'm ready for Shirl's ass today. Or at least her mouth. I pour a big glass for myself, and an even bigger one for her, hoping to keep her lips fruitfully occupied, at least part of the time.

I hope in vain.

"How you just let them boys run loose 'round here? Ain't you 'fraid?" Her tone lets me know that if I had any sense, I would be.

"'Fraid of what, Shirl," I ask.

"Some ol' somebody snatch 'em up, and you wouldn't even know they was gone."

I have to laugh. "Anyone snatches them boys won't last an hour, 'specially not if they have to feed 'em. And since when you seen somebody 'round here that you *didn't* know well enough to talk about 'em like a dog?"

"Hmmph. Ain't funny. Gots to be careful even of folks you do know. Plenty of folks 'round here, I wouldn't put it past 'em to try something. That VidaMae — "

I can't stand it. "Shirl. Why you hate VidaMae so much?"

"I just don't trust her."

"Naw, this is past don't trust. Hell, I don't trust Miz Lucy. VidaMae do something to you?"

"I...she..." Shirl scrunches up her face. "Why you axe me that?"

"Why you so down on VidaMae?"

"Selfish heifer."

"You talk about her, but you ain' never talk *to* her, so how you know?"

"She just is."

"Why?"

Silence.

"Shirl," I say. "Who's your mama, Shirl?"

"I ain't got one," she snarls.

"Okay. Shirl, who's *my* mama?" Maybe my mama, I add, silently.

"She…you…"

I wait. I'm good at it.

"You…" Shirl's voice breaks apart. "You gon' be like the rest of us," she whispers. Naw I ain't, I think.

"You *s'pposed* to be." Shirl's as bad as Miz Lucy. Her whisper's edge could cut glass. "How come you get to walk 'round here all regular, and we gots to be…to stay like…" Them crab claw hands wavin' in my face again. I snap.

"Y'all the ones all the time hangin' round VidaMae."

"*I ain't. I hate her!*"

"Fine, but don't hate on me. I tried. I can't fix…everything, but I did try."

"You didn't do *shit*."

Stung, I holler back. "I got us a place."

"*This ain't our place!*" Shirl screamin' now.

And we both just shut up right there, 'cos it's true. VidaMae and me and Shirl and Precious and Tyco; even Glory and Honor. We don't really belong here. And Miz Lucy…well, she's got her own agenda and I 'spect it ain't in nobody's interest but her own. Life ain't supposed t' hold still.

"You don't have to stay," I say. "You could go. We all could."

"But…but then…how you know what Vida — what Mama gon' do?"

"I don't," I say.

"I don't…" says Shirl after a bit, "I don't want you to end up like us." It's the nicest, softest thing I've ever heard Shirl say.

"What you wanna do, Shirl?" I ain't even stressed no more, and it's like floating. Shirl twist up her face at me like she mad again. Then all of the meanness kinda wash out of her. I understand. It takes too much energy to hold all that hurt.

"Go h-h-home…" Shirl cryin' like there ain't already enough salt in the world, but she makin' sense.

I drag her wheelchair down the steps and help her get settled before crawling under the space beneath the porch. It's almost cool under there, and the dirt between my fingers is as soft as cake flour. Shirl still cryin'. It sounds almost like music. I haul myself out 'fore I'm tempted to stay. The conch shell feels warm and heavy in my palm, and uneven, like somethin' sloshing 'round inside it. I toss the shell and Miz Lucy's keys over my shoulder as I walk back toward Shirl. Hear a clink and a crack. Don't even look back.

"You don't haf' t' push," Shirl sniffs. I do, anyway.

VI

VidaMae walks heavily through the late afternoon, heart and womb full up, leaving tracks in the softened tar and dirt past the road to the docks, all the way down to sandy curve of deserted beach. White foam washes over metal slats threaded with leather straps and a wheelchair abandoned on its side. VidaMae kicks off her shoes and walks right into the water, relishing its coolness against her ankles, her thighs; shedding her blue jacket and white blouse now soaked and indistinguishable from water and foam.

Mama!

Mama's here.

"Mama's sorry. Ty? Precious? Mama's so very sorry."

I know, Mama. I know, Tyco, mannish, comforting.

VidaMae hears singing from far off, and down deep, but can't make out the words. "Shirl?" She calls. "Baby girl?" VidaMae dives in the direction of the song, glimpses a flash of silver scales and landlocked legs that have found their purpose, surfaces smiling with her hair streaming and shell-encrusted, water droplets beading like pearls, the blue drawstring pants drifting off below.

Look at me, Mama. Look! Precious arcs up out of the water, splashing like a dolphin, naked, glistening brown, and laughing. VidaMae laughs, too. Baby boy! He wheels and lunges, a bloody raw stump mudpuppy with a screaming mouth and glistening teeth. *See me, Mama? See me? SEE ME???*

"I see you. Come here." VidaMae leans into the rending embrace of soft, angry flipper arms. Precious' teeth tear at her breasts; blood flows like milk or the tears leaking from the corners of VidaMae's eyes, brine dissolving in brine. Shirl's voice is closer now, crooning in VidaMae's ears as rough scales abrade her skin, claws and pincers grasp, pierce, rip away flesh to make space for the anemones and seaweed to root. VidaMae closes her eyes, turns her pain into a harmony hummed deep in her chest, rocks in wave rhythm as she pulls her babies close.

I love you, Mama. VidaMae squints up into Tyco's eyes. The sun behind him makes a halo of light around his wet curls. His lips are rounded, protuberant. VidaMae raises her chin, offers her face to fully jellyfish stingray kisses, poisonous and sweet. Tentacles wrap around her, attaching with persistent suction. VidaMae clamps her legs together and they fuse, lengthen, her feet turning outward, expanding and unfurling like wings. VidaMae slaps her broad tail against the water's surface, sending up a shower of sparkling droplets. Laughing, she sweeps her children into a crushing embrace and dives them down together, moving with the tides, streaming life in her wake.

VII

I'm left here to wait. Like I say, I'm good at it.

The sun is a big orange ball falling down behind the water. Mr. Briscoe's boat is a grey-blue silhouette against a sky the color of ripening peaches. The chug-chug of its motor makes its own kind of music, but I can still hear Mama and Shirl singing.

I smile, picturing Miz Lucy's store unminded, my towel folded neatly on the red plastic couch, the blades on the black metal fan and the busted clock spinning to themselves; Miz Lucy coming along, finally, to find the key ring and the cracked shell on the steps. For a minute, I swear I smell them nasty Lucky Strikes. Then a quick breeze fills my nose with the smells of machine oil, salt and sea flesh.

I see my boys on deck, pullin' in the nets, workin' hard. I wave just in case they can see me. Glory and Honor, comin'. ∽

The Heart of the Song

PAN MORIGAN

~ WE WAGON-TRAVELERS lost the whole world and regained it in the turning of a song. We tell a story about it. Listen:

There was one who lived with the Red-Wheel Clan so long ago, beloved by everybody in her camp. Whatever she had she shared. If she had a piece of bread or a fruit, each had a bite, however small. If she had a bowl of soup, she passed it around so everybody could enjoy a spoonful. And she studied. She sat with her Grannymair and her Oldies daily, to learn what they had to teach of life. Her memory was prodigious and marvelous. She learned the many languages of her Clan, the stories and lore of other times. Most especially she memorized songs. "Songs make the suns shift and turn, the moons burn," she said. She loved to sing.

This girl was not beautiful to look at. Some needed to say it — those who cared for such matters. Her hair was the color of wood and ever tangled. Her clothes were ragged and patched. Her feet were big, calloused. Her eyes were deep-set and solemn, like those of an Oldie who had seen too many merciless days. This was troublesome in such a young face. Still, everybody in the Clan and Wagon-Travelers everywhere desired her company. She was generous to a fault and always singing.

One winter, a terrible wind raced down from the cliffs of Gik into the valley where the Clan was camped. The wind howled around camp, a shrieking haint, leaving hard, sparkling frost on every surface it touched.

Folk huddled in their wagons to keep from freezing. The caravans rocked in the wind, groaning. It was impossible to build a fire or cook. When somebody did manage to create a fitful blaze, there was nothing to put in the pot. People hungered.

Well-armed Mercenairs were in a bad mood, raiding often. They tore through the wagons, searching for coin or bread. In the end they stole horses. The people heard the Mercenairs carousing and drinking on the hills and they smelled roasting meat. Mercenairs liked horse-flesh.

The Red-Wheel Clan fled, moving further and further into the wilds. They trudged through mud and rain and swamp, searching for refuge. Soon they found themselves in a thick, snarled forest far from any town or city. Oldies set up camp, while youngies looked for kindling, for nuts or roots to dig from the ground and eat, for small game to catch in snares and cook. The people had no luck. They returned home with empty baskets. The firewood they gathered was soaked through.

Snow fell night and day. The snow kept falling until it covered the wheels of the wagons. All the world was silent, bathed in deathly blue light. The people were mired. They starved. Some nursed fevers. Perhaps the Clan would not survive until spring.

The kind girl did all she could to help. She boiled snow to make tea from twigs cut from brush and tree. She sang to the children to soothe them when hunger made them fret. She massaged the chilled hands of her Oldies. She told the people tales to keep their spirits up.

One day as twilight gathered, the snow eased. The girl went out the door of her snowbound wagon. She stood at the steps of her caravan and spoke to the spirits of winter, begging them to have pity on her Clan. The cold air was white with her breath. Her tears turned to ice on her cheeks.

The cold sky was faraway and uncaring. The cold wind had no answers for her.

The girl heard a voice crying somewhere beyond the trees. Fearing that a child had gone out in the dim light and gotten lost, she ventured into the snowdrifts. She struggled a long way, her heavy skirts wet with snow and her boots soaked through. She followed the weeping voice. Soon the suns closed their sad eyes, leaving the world naked and alone. The moons did not rise for fear of the frozen darkness. The snow shone, impenetrable, ruthless blue. Sky unfolded in deepest purple-black, mourning the spring which had fled far, far, searching for joy and ease.

The temperature dropped. The girl's feet were stone-numb and she could not stop shuddering. She called to the child, saying, "Stay still so that I might find you!" The cry moved here and there as if the lost one wandered to and fro through the forest, just beyond the girl's reach.

The girl knew she had walked too long. If she did not get back to her caravan fast or find shelter, she would die of cold. She wondered if the crying voice was that of a haint luring her into the other world. She gazed up at the stars to get her bearings. It was useless. She did not recognize the constellations overhead. How far had she walked? She was completely lost. She hurried north through a dark grove, reaching unfamiliar hills and cliffs. She would look for shelter amongst the rocks and brush, however bleak. Perhaps she would dig a hole.

The girl found a cave in the side of a high, stony hill. The crying voice came from there. She only hesitated a moment. If it was a haint, still, the cave would provide shelter. She ignored her fear of hungering bears and entities unknown, following the crying voice through the dark cave-mouth. She found a lofty cavern inside and gasped at the sight of a massive Earth-dragon. It lifted its huge head weakly, opening heavy-lidded white eyes.

"Someone has answered my call." Its scales were silvery white. It was white all over, like the snow. Even the fire burning in the middle of the cavern was white and gave off no heat. Icy air swirled all around.

"Who are you?"

The girl did not move, hoping the creature's white eyes were blind and that she might slip away.

"Do not turn your back to me." It spoke in a voice of dry leaves and wind. "Instead, warm yourself at my fire."

The girl said, "Your fire is no comfort to me, for it is cold."

"It is also no comfort to me," the Earth-dragon said. "If you sing a song, the fire will burn hot again and save us both."

"I will sing a song for you," the girl said, hoping this act of kindness would convince the Earth-dragon to grant safe passage. Her Grannymair would be worried for her.

"I must warn you that if you sing the song, you will forget it just as if you had never known it at all."

"I will sing a song for you nonetheless." The girl thought, I will go home and my oldies will teach me the song again. "It is no loss."

The girl chose a beautiful song about a summer Wagon-Traveler gathering. All the caravans and Clans had joined together in camp. They chose a spot high in the hills around the cliffs of Gik. A fire was built and instruments were brought out. Two young people of the Purple-Wheel Clan danced together and fell in love.

As the girl sang, the fire grew brighter. She could see the caravans and the cliffs of Gik in the white flames. A boy and girl danced to the music of fiddles and drums. The fire took on the colors of life, pale green, yellow, and orange. It grew warmer. And the dragon's scales were burnished in golden light.

When she was finished the dragon said, "You have a very beautiful voice. I wish that you would sing to me through the night."

"I must go home. My people are worried about me."

"If you remain this night, I will reward you and give you anything you wish."

"I wish that my people would have enough to eat and wood to light their fires and never be persecuted anymore. I wish that the snow would finally stop and spring remain with all its abundance. Nobody can give me that."

"I can. But you must sing for me until dawn. And understand, you will forget each of the songs that you sing."

The girl thought to herself that even if she forgot the songs, it would be worth it. If her people might only find peace and safety and food to eat. So she sang. And as she sang, the fire grew hotter and hotter. The Earth-dragon's scales turned gold, then crimson. Its eyes became brilliant, smoldering coals. And the girl forgot each song as she sang it, as if she had never known it at all. She grew weary, as though her strength was sucked into the flames. At least she was not cold any longer.

Finally dawn came. The snow had stopped. The girl could see shafts of pale sunlight slanting through the cave-mouth. The dragon thanked her for her songs and said, "You are free to return home."

The girl stood to go. The dragon said, "Drink from the pool before you go or your people will not recognize you."

There was a small pool at the narrow end of the cavern, and the girl stumbled to it, so weary, she could hardly lift her legs. She bent to drink at the pool and saw that she had been transformed into a dragon, white as snow. She drank, and the water was not cool or wet, but bitter fire on her tongue. When she looked again, she had taken her true shape once more.

The dragon went to the mouth of the cave and took wing into the sky. The girl watched it go. "Where to?" She called.

"I am going to hunt and eat. Don't worry, I won't eat your people."

The girl took the measure of the sun and wind and knew which way she must walk to get home. She went and by the time she reached home, it was twilight. She found her people celebrating. Long tables were set under the trees. The snow had melted away. Leaves and flowers unfurled and grasses grew high. The wind was warm and sweet, as if spring had never been conquered. The tables were set with platters of rich and delicious foods. Her people were feasting and singing.

The girl was very happy, yet so weary she crawled into her wagon and slept for three days without eating anything herself. As she slept, her Grannymair stroked her tangled hair and wept.

When the girl awoke, she saw that snow was falling again, a dense wall of white. The wind was fiercer than ever. The food was gone. She knew that the dragon was summoning her. She said to her family, "I have to go and do not follow me." Her family was sad. Still, they knew she was a sensible girl and so they trusted her decision.

When she reached the cavern, the Earth-dragon thanked her for coming and told her that if she agreed to sing every night, her Clan would never again know hunger or fear. They would not want for anything. All she had to do was sing.

"I need fodder for my fire," the Earth-dragon said. "And there is nothing finer than your songs. Remember you will forget them once you have sung them. It is only fair to remind you of this."

The girl sang for the dragon night after night and in so doing turned herself into a dragon. Each morning she drank from the bitter pool, hurried home, and slept. She no longer sat with her Oldies learning the lore of the Wagon-Travelers. She no longer told stories or sang songs on moonlit nights, or entertained her family and all the children of the Clan. She was too weary of singing. When children asked her for a certain song or lullaby, she told them she did not know it any longer. Soon people forgot the sound of her voice and did not ask her for songs. She thought to herself, some day soon I will sit with my Grannymair and learn all the songs once again.

That time never came and never came.

After a while, the girl felt too tired to walk all the way home each day. She did not drink the fiery medicine from the pool. She remained in the shape of a snow-white creature, sleeping in the cave all day while the Earth-dragon went hunting. "Don't worry, I will not eat your people," it always said as it lifted wing into the sky.

This went on for a long, long time. The dragon who was once a girl sang hundreds of songs and then forgot them. Finally one morning, she realized that she only had one song left inside her. It was the oldest song in the world. The opening verse described the first two people who ever existed, two beautiful lovers from whom all of humanity descended. The second and third verses described their love and their children who peopled all time and all space. The last verse described the people of today, who would not exist but for the love of those first two.

The girl lay worrying in the cave that day. She could not sleep or rest.

She did not want to sing this song to the dragon. She was afraid to do so. At the hour of setting suns the dragon-girl drank of the pool and became herself again. She had to drink and drink, the fiery water burning her lips and throat.

The transformation back to human shape was very painful, and still, one of her arms was missing. In its place was the diaphanous, silver wing of a dragon folded against her ribs. Worse, her eyes, once black as obsidian, remained white. She left the cave and was blinded by the red horizon. She shaded her white eyes with her one remaining hand and hurried home. She hid her wing beneath her shawl and did not look at anybody for fear her strange eyes would give fright. She ran straight to her Grannymair and fell into her arms weeping. She confessed everything. Then she said, "Please, please teach me the songs again, so that I might bring something to the dragon tonight — anything but the oldest song in the world!"

The girl's Grannymair, ancient and bent, told the girl to sit by the fire. She brought her soup and fed her. Then she sat with the girl's head in her lap and stroked her tangled hair. She spoke to her very gently, so as not to alarm her. She told the girl a story. And the meaning of the story was this: I do not know any songs. We have forgotten all the songs. Nobody knows them anymore. You have given them all away. And the dragon has used them for firewood.

The girl sat up, her white eyes wide. "We must go to the other Clans, then, and they will know the songs. We will learn them again. Let's go right now, quickly!"

Grannymair said, "There is nobody left. The dragon, your Master, has hunted them down and eaten them all. We are the only ones still living."

"If I sing the song of the first people, Grannymair, I fear the dragon will go hunting through our past. It may devour the first mother and the first father. And there will be nobody left in the world throughout all time, for none of us will have been born. Everything will be destroyed."

"Then, my daughter, you must not sing that song," Grannymair said.

"What can I do? If I do not sing the dragon will hunt us down. We will no longer be protected."

"We must consult with your brother."

So the girl and her Grannymair went to the brother. He was very happy to see his sister again for he had missed her. However, he grieved to see her one-armed, with a dragon-wing, eyes so weary and white. He said, "You rest, sister, while Grannymair and I walk together."

On return, he said, "I understand what I must do and I agree."

So Grannymair made a powerful potion from the crimson berries that grow on a certain thorny bush. The brother drank a large bowlful of the hot red drink.

The girl thought, this is good. Such a drink will make him superbly strong. We can fight the dragon while it is famished and weak. The two said goodbye to their Grannymair, kissing her wrinkled, brown cheeks. They marched through the thick forests to the dragon's cave, the girl leading the way.

She entered the cavern first. It was frigid.

The dragon was waiting impatiently for songs. Its scales were white, its voice tremulous. "You are late," it hissed. "Now sing, as I am chilled and hungry."

Her brother strode into the cavern. "Sister, hide." He drew both long spear and sharp blade.

The dragon rose up, spitting white fire and lashing its armored tail.

"You betrayed me, girl." It coughed, heavy-headed. "I will take you for my supper!" Then it sat down. "Sing to me first," it said. "I will spare you. But I will not spare him, the foolish boy with his silly toys."

"I will not sing my last song for you."

The dragon was enraged. Its eyes were dead ash. "I will fight your brother. If I lose the contest, you may go free and fend for yourselves in this cruel world. If I win, the boy will be my supper tonight and you must sing to me forever or follow him to the netherworld."

The girl's brother landed a few hard blows beneath the dragon's golden scales. The dragon only laughed. The wounds did not slow the beast or even cause pain. The brother was outmatched. He fought until his legs trembled and his arms hung, broken and useless. He knelt before the dragon and offered himself.

The girl screamed out to him, throwing sharp rocks into the dragon's face. Why would her brother not try harder?

The dragon wrapped its armored tail around the boy's body. It crushed his bones and took bites of his flesh, crunching on ribs and skull, drinking warm blood.

The girl huddled by the pool, sobbing. What sort of plan was this that her Grannymair and brother had hatched?

The dragon said, "Now you must sing to me, as agreed." She thought, I will die first. Before she could reply, the dragon wailed with pain. It pawed the air, huge head twisting on its thick, scaly neck. It writhed and rolled and fell to the hard stone floor, dead.

The girl realized that the red-berry brew her Grannymair had made was dragon poison. Drinking it, her brother sacrificed himself for his sister, his Clan, for the lovers at the beginning of time, and for all people, forever.

The girl left the cave. She walked miles and miles, full of grief. She pondered why her brother had agreed to this act. Could they not have found another way? Weeks later, torn, tattered, and starving, she returned to her people.

"Why did you let him do it?" She asked her Grannymair. "The Earth-Dragon could have taken me instead." Grannymair gripped the girl's one, cold, trembling hand and said, "It was your brother's gift to you. His choice."

Spring finally returned. The people dug for roots and hunted small game as they did long ago. No fine table was set for them. No kingly food was provided. Neither did winter last forever. The people traveled in their wagons, following the rivers and seasons. They survived. Yet life was not as before. The people had no songs to sing any more, only that final, oldest one, the song of the first lovers. They sang it over and over, but it no longer gave joy. Everyone felt sad and empty. Even the children did not laugh or play. In time the people forgot how to lift their voices. Life was without savor, spice, or beauty.

One day in fall, with the leaves raining down, Dragon-Girl left camp, saying, "I am not fit to live amongst you. I won't come home until I've found all our songs once more. My people, I invoke the Covenant of the Ghost." In this way she banished herself. Nobody was allowed to follow her.

The girl wandered over the whole world from top to bottom and side to side. She shielded her white eyes from the angry suns and carried her one wing hidden close to her ribs. With such a wing she could not fly nor did she wish to. She found no people living in the world and nobody to teach her a song. The dragon had eaten all the tribes except her own one. Even the birds were silent.

Years passed and the girl grew deeply lonely. Solitude scored her face and hurt her bones. One day, stretched beside a river in desperate pain, she lifted her voice and sang out. The notes came like rain, like hail, fast, rough, and loud. The forests and seas stopped breathing, listening to this strange cry from the heart. Dragon-Girl grieved and sang her grief. She was afraid, so she sang fear. She was hungry and thirsty. She sang hunger, sang thirst. She was lost and so she sang the roads, the hills, the deserts; the winds and tides. She was a girl and also a dragon. She sang blood, regret, and fire.

Over many years, she made new songs. Making, she dreamed and remembered. Dreaming and remembering, even the old songs came back to her — those she had fed to the dragon and forgotten. What she could not remember whole, she stitched together, patches of song, strips and bits and scraps of song. In this way she sang her days, her nights, her years.

In time, as Dragon-Girl sang her mended songs, the people of the world sprang back to life. Through her singing, the dead, silent world was made green and beautiful again. Yet she herself was not healed. The strange white eyes and the wing of a dragon reminded her of what she had sold away. And no matter how passionately she sang, her brother never came back to life.

Finally, after many years of wandering, she went home an old Granny-mair. The children sat at her feet, eager to learn the hundreds of songs she brought with her and the stories of her travels.

She said, "We must snatch our songs from the jaws of the dragon."

Us Wagon-Travelers have kept that belief ever since.

And she said, "It matters who we are, even when we're cold, hungry, and frightened. We don't trade who we are for bread or triumph."

SING ON, Ursula K. Le Guin. I am grateful to you for valuing the average folk in your stories who struggle to find creativity, a voice, and freedom within themselves and within their communities. Thank you for making much of singers and writers, for drawing portraits of painters and weavers, for taking note of dancers and dreamers, and for loving the stubborn, the seekers. Your work has said to me, yes, you are real, even if the world says, "no, you are not." Your wonderful stories proclaim, yes, do not give up, keep singing, even if the world says, "what is a song worth?"

Thank you is too small a word for a lifetime of work spun of love and for the work surely yet to come.

And so I'll sing on too, write and draw in company with my beloved artists' collective, Beyon' Dusa, which is ten years old this year and counting, despite all predictions to the contrary.

With love and good wishes on your birthday,

PAN MORIGAN
SINGER-SONGWRITER/COMPOSER/WRITER/PERFORMER
OF FLORENCE MASSACHUSETTS VIA CHICAGO AND CANADA ⌇

[Untitled]

ELLEN EADES

IN COLLEGE, my best friend (and, serendipitously, freshman roommate…
thank you Reed College dorm placement people!) and I were fanatic Le
Guin fans and bookworms. We went to hear a talk by Le Guin at nearby
Lewis & Clark College, and one day when procrastinating about my
David Hume paper, I produced the following doggerel:

> Higgledy Piggledy
> Ursula K. Le Guin
> Writes of a world where
> Either is both.
>
> How'd she come up with such
> Ambisexterity?
> Guess when she wrote it, her
> Mind was in dothe.

Thank you, Ursula, for getting me through my college years with my
sense of humor intact.

Marginalia from *The Left Hand of Darkness*

PAUL PREUSS

THE LEFT HAND OF DARKNESS was my introduction to Ursula's fiction and my reintroduction to science fiction generally, which I'd let slide since my teens. Reading it set off a mental explosion: by God, this is *about* something, the richness and complexity of human desire, fear, courage, obligation, love, honor…politics and philosophy and folklore and music… sex and what it makes of us…and oh yes, suspense and adventure and an epic journey and a strange planet and faster-than-light communication and all that neat stuff too.

Sex wasn't the first thing that struck me, which seems strange now. The novel was recommended by an anthropologist friend; from the daughter of Kroebers I expected anthropology, and that's what I got. A planet where everybody was both sexes but only occasionally one or the other seemed a terrific way to convey the superficial oddness of an unfamiliar culture and how it can disguise the fundamental constants of human nature. In other words, I missed the point.

Nevertheless I was so enthusiastic about all the other stuff — astonishing characters, nail-biting plot, extreme setting — that I secured an option on the novel and, with my friend Richard Chew, who'd recently finished editing *One Flew Over the Cuckoo's Nest* and with whom I'd written a couple of scripts, went to meet Ursula while she was visiting the ancestral Kroeber home in the Berkeley Hills. My memory is of a

Maybeck manor house made of old redwood, dark and brooding. Out of the shadows emerged a woman smoking a pipe.

Written with due respect for Ursula's warnings ("No masculine-feminine pronouns; if I had it to do over, they wouldn't be in the book"), Richard's and my script bounced around Hollywood for a year or so and then sank. Meanwhile I started reading the rest of the Le Guin corpus. Plus a lot of other science fiction and fantasy and whatever; it seems that, after all, there were many other writers of the suspect genres whose books were about something: Čapek. Dick. Zamyatin. Lem. Borges. And more, closer to home. But nothing quite like Le Guin.

In *The Dispossessed*, an intricate narrative runs backward and forward in time and cuts between scientific and political systems, an electric display of scholarship and virtuosity. But what sticks in the mind are vivid scenes of the breakdown of rational social systems under the pressure of unformed human character — communitarian bullies and cheats, smooth technocratic liars, a child locked up in the dark. *The Wizard of Earthsea*'s brooding dragons are so elementally crafty and strong, and from the beginning the wizard school is so deftly evoked, as if inked in *sumi-e*, that *Earthsea*, together with *The Lord of the Rings*, pretty much spoiled me for fantasy (I never got past the first page of Harry Potter). But the meat of the book is Ged and his shadow, eerie as Conrad's secret sharer, wrestling for his soul like Jacob with the angel.

As a storyteller Ursula often employs an interesting device. In *The Dispossessed*, Einstein's General Theory of Relativity spins into Shevek's General Temporal Theory, in which signals, if not objects, certainly travel faster than the speed of light. In *The Left Hand of Darkness*, Zen satori becomes the Foretellers' "perfect uselessness of knowing the answer to the wrong question." These aren't trivial inversions; she mines paradox for intellectual insights and for the engines of character and plot, viz *Dispossessed*'s retroparallel structure. An impulse to flip unquestioned assumptions and self-evident common sense on their heads is what makes *The Left Hand of Darkness* possible.

As a stylist, this form-changing impulse shows itself as an ability to slip effortlessly from one point of view to another, or to review the same incident or theme from multiple vantages in time. The resonance of *The Left Hand of Darkness* comes partly from what Ursula might easily have left out, Gethen's myths and songs and legends, most tellingly the legend of Estraven the Traitor.

The same fluid precision informs her dialogue; sometimes she does it all at once, as in *Lavinia*. In a shadowy encounter the poet who will create Lavinia (inadequately) describes the future to her: "The king's daughter ran through the house with blazing hair, scattering sparks and smoke. And war and glory followed her." She asks, "Why must there be war?" Vergil replies, "Oh, Lavinia, what a woman's question that is! Because men are men."

Elmore Leonard and Ursula Le Guin are about as different as two storytellers can get, but when it comes to dialogue they practice the same craft. Leonard quotes a Steinbeck character: "I don't like to have nobody tell me what the guy looks like. I want to figure out what he looks like from the way he talks." In her essay "From Elfland to Poughkeepsie," Le Guin asks, "Just because a writer gets the tone of a conversation a bit wrong… does that disqualify his book as a fantasy?…is that so important?" and she answers, "I think it is."

"Elfland," which is about language, says as much about Ursula's own character as it does about how she makes characters come alive: "Plain language is the noblest of all," she writes, and, "Nobody who says, 'I told you so' has ever been, or will ever be, a hero."

How plainspoken she is I learned when I later got to know her in person. The first time I tried a novel of my own, she agreed to read the draft ("You cheated — we got interested in the character in the first chapter, then she vanished and never came back"), and she has done me the same service a couple of times since. Her advice tends to be straight-forward: "This needs to be a hundred pages shorter," or "Leave out the Greek." Reading another writer's manuscript is about as generous as an author can be, but pithy suggestions have hardly been the limit of Ursula's generosity. There are other fine writers, photographers, painters, people in the cattle business that my wife, Debra, and I wouldn't know if she and Charles weren't delighted to share.

Most of what I know about writing comes from reading Le Guin. Some years after Richard and I first attempted a script I wrote her to say I'd been thinking about *The Left Hand of Darkness* and wondered if she were game for a collaboration. (Let me kill the suspense right now. Despite indications of interest no script was sold, and as of now no movie is in the works.) Over the next decade she and I worked on several dis-tinct versions, each more explicit about sex. The final one was enriched with scenes, some only hinted at in the book, in which Gethenian chil-dren play crucial plot roles. That was the best of the imaginary movies we wrote. I still browse it with pleasure.

Yet despite all that's now technically possible, I wonder if an adequate movie of this story can ever be made. The problem is that the essence of film, no matter how overlaid by trickery and computer graphics, is, well…

one could call it photorealism, but the word I want is more like evidence.

You can get away with things in words that you can't get away with in film. Alice Sheldon was James Tiptree for years, although not without sparking speculation and argument. In film (or high-resolution video) a man or woman — or child, after a certain age, which may be very young — no matter how well made-up, no matter how skilled an actor, no matter how unknown to the public, radiates sexual identity frame by frame, even when unaware, even when trying not to. At the core of *The Left Hand of Darkness* is a grappling with sexual identity, and what it makes of us, far more fundamental than anything conceivable outside of written science fiction. In the familiar world, androgyny may be empathetic, heroic even — as in Jeffrey Eugenides's *Middlesex*, say — but it stays on the fringe, while on Gethen, androgyny is so matter of fact it's less than trivial.

Having said that, I hope I'm wrong, and that someday someone will find a way to turn Ursula's story, with its astonishing premise and the strong, simple, passionate lessons that rise from it — not to mention its ripping good suspense and action — into a movie with even a fraction of the power of her incomparable novel. Until then, luckily, we have the novel itself, and many generations of fortunate readers will have it as well.

A Few Things I Know About Ursula

MOLLY GLOSS

PEOPLE MEETING ME for the first time, upon hearing that I write science fiction, sometimes will say that they don't read science fiction. Of course this doesn't ever surprise me, because, after all, many people don't read science fiction, and there's a way of saying this — quietly apologetic — as an explanation for having too many books piled up on one's bedside table, and not enough time for reading. There's just no graceful way to say, "I'm sorry I haven't gotten around to reading your books yet," and they might be thinking it's more politic to say: "Oh, I am sorry, I don't read science fiction, but I've heard your work is very good." There is some trouble with this tack, though, as an explanation, as an apology, to the writer of science fiction. Here's the problem: When someone says they don't read science fiction, they seem to be saying they haven't, in fact, read any science fiction.

This makes me think of the great numbers of native Oregonians (do people from other states do this too?) who take a kind of perverse pride in declaring their dislike of California. They often seem to be saying that California, like science fiction, is a place they already know they wouldn't like if they ever went there, which they never have. They seem to be saying they've crossed it off their list, not on the basis of considerate, careful reading of the travels books, the maps, the texts, but on bad press, of which science fiction and California have had more than their share. I've known some Californians who, in certain situations, denied they were from California, and science fiction writers who believed that the only way to get literary respectability was to deny the science fiction label. But one of the things I know about Ursula is that she writes science fiction, although not only science fiction, and that she is, herself, though long an Oregonian, originally from California, and never has been shy about saying so.

In fact, here is something else I know about Ursula. Not only does she try to make her own judgments on the basis of considerate, careful reading of the texts and travel books, but sometimes she takes a kind of perverse pleasure in embracing the very thing receiving the bad press of the moment. She has been, for instance, and I believe is at this very moment, a flaming liberal, an outspoken feminist, an abortion rights activist, a civil libertarian, a loud and unswerving opponent of censorship, an environmentalist, and an enemy of the OCA, which is Oregon's local pack of ultra-right-wing, anti-gay paranoiacs.

Here are a few more things I know about Ursula. She has been, in one way or another, at one time or another, a Taoist, a Utopian, and a pacifist anarchist. She's a teacher, one of our best — a teacher who doesn't pontificate or indoctrinate or evangelize, though there's no denying she's a woman of strong opinions. She's funny, she laughs easily, she can be a wiseacre. She's a reluctant flyer — she favors low-tech traveling, by train. She was slow to boot up, slow to forsake her old fossil of an Underwood, though by now she's racing along pretty low and fast on her Mac and has become a committed aficionado of email. She's a housewife-poet. She was a graduate-school-dropout-stay-at-home-mother.

And she has brought these experiences, this consciousness, to her work as a writer.

In many of her novels and stories, her characters seem to be groping toward an understanding that you must sometimes stand up and be counted, if silence is not to collude with injustice. Some of her characters seem to be seeking a deeper connection to the place where they live, places that are often sad, proud, absurd, peculiar. Some of her characters are themselves eccentrics, invalids, oddities, exiles. In her novels and stories there are communities that have survived tragedies and have reshaped themselves around the losses, as well as communities mostly beneficent toward their members and their place. What you will not find in her work is sentimentality. These are communities in Emerson's sense of the word — places where the complexities, and the suffering, and the work of belonging are fully faced and acknowledged.

The literary world can conjure a landscape, a community, call it up into imagination; and thus being made real, it becomes a place worth caring about. And if the writer has brought her whole self to a novel, then as a reader, when we're swept along to the place inside the story and participate in it, live in it, allow our lives to be merged with the lives of those people, we learn from the experience, we're changed by it.

One thing I know about Ursula is that she brings her whole self to her writing. When we read her novels, her stories, her poetry, we are enriched by them, and we begin to see ways we can inhabit, or reinhabit, our world. Her wisdom is that she understands: becoming a member of a community is not about making space for yourself, it's about learning to listen to the stories around you; it's about being alert, open to what's out there, so that the voices of your neighbors will give you the chance to become a neighbor yourself, and then to begin to tell your own stories.

I am grateful to Ursula for many personal reasons to do with friendship and generosity, advice, encouragement; but I admire her for the simple reason that her life is an example to me, and that her books have become, for me, as for many others, polestars, compasses — Michelin guides — not to California, but to the farthest borders of consciousness, where, in the embrace of words, we understand something that transcends words.

The community of writers and readers is enriched by her very presence among us.

My Life with Le Guin

SARAH LEFANU

URSULA K. LE GUIN was the subject of my first-ever published writing, in the feminist magazine *Spare Rib* in 1975. I wrote about *The Left Hand of Darkness* and the newly-published *The Dispossessed*. Reading the piece again now I catch a glimpse of a young woman searching for some clear lineaments of a radical sexual politics; she commended Le Guin for "touching on the dialectics between modes of production, sexuality and consciousness," but complained that "the norm remains a heterosexual one." That young woman was made anxious by finding *The Left Hand of Darkness* "highly readable"; in those days of struggle, I seem to remember, the more palatable the politics the more suspicious one was of them.

I don't think my younger self yet realised that the rhythm and the flow of a piece of prose, the pleasurable sounds picked up by a reader's inner ear, are the fruits of a writer's tussle with language. Nor did that young woman appreciate the extraordinary range of registers in both books that create whole worlds with their laws and legends, their customs and conflicts, their shared beliefs and individual voices. She didn't want to be seduced by the hearth-tales in *The Left Hand of Darkness*, the myths and stories of love and betrayal amidst Gethen's frozen lakes and rock-hard earth, that provide not just a rich, complex, and credible history for this invented society but a personal history for the characters in it. She viewed with suspicion what she called Le Guin's "realism."

But I'm not going to disown that young woman. I take Earthsea's Tenar as my model, Tenar who was once Arha of Atuan, and later became Goha the farmwife of Gont. At one point Tenar — or is it Goha? — reflects on all the selves she's been, and acknowledges them all. I think of how we bring a different self to each new reading of a favourite book, and I acknowledge and accept that sternly political-critical young woman writing in 1975, my younger self.

It was the bold skewedness of *The Left Hand of Darkness* that first made me think about and want to explore the parallels between a feminist and a science fictional worldview. It was *The Left Hand of Darkness* that led me on to other writers: to Suzy McKee Charnas, to Joanna Russ, to the late great James Tiptree Jr. Later, when I read the novel in the 1990s, I saw what I hadn't seen before in Genly Ai's emotional confusions around the hermaphroditic Gethenians: an exploration of masculinity and its discontents. And when I wrote about it again, in 2003 for the *Guardian,* I was particularly struck by Le Guin's picture of the jitteriness and para-noia that infects people when their countries are sliding swiftly down the precipitous road to war.

Readers as much as writers are shaped by their times, and bring their own preoccupations and concerns — their baggage of self — to their reading of a book. Ursula K. Le Guin illuminated this for me by her own practice, and alerted me to the pleasure of surprise that is re-reading's gift. She revisited *The Left Hand of Darkness* seven years after its first publication with her commentary "Is Gender Necessary?" and returned once more, with a commentary on that commentary, a decade or so later. And she has returned to Earthsea again and again. At the end of the third book in the trilogy, *The Farthest Shore,* Ged was on the dragon Kalessin's back, flying from Roke, back to his home island of Gont. Seventeen years separate the publication of *The Farthest Shore* and *Tehanu: The Last Book of Earthsea*, while in Earthsea barely a moment has passed. Ged is still on Kalessin's back. They are about to land on a cliff-edge on Gont. Barely a moment, but the vision of Earthsea is changed utterly.

Ursula K. Le Guin has always offered not so much a challenge to her readers as an invitation:

> Read this again.
> See this again.

Or to use what she calls the "invaluable word" she borrowed from the poet Adrienne Rich: revision this.

Ursula K. Le Guin revisioned Earthsea. The result was to open up what had seemed to be a finished trilogy to the possibility of change and growth. She knocked a hole in Earthsea, and let the heroics fast run out of it. She gave us the feminist masterpiece, *Tehanu*. Then she went on from there to give us *The Other Wind*, and *Tales from Earthsea*, which are tales "for those who have liked or think they might like the place, and who are willing to accept these hypotheses: things change; authors and wizards are not always to be trusted; nobody can explain a dragon."

Things change: writers, readers, and books.

Reading and re-reading Ursula's books has been and will remain for me a lasting, and changing, source of pleasure, as each new reading elicits a different reading self.

A few years ago my son, who's now twenty-six, said anxiously one day: "What would we do if Ursula Le Guin stopped writing?" She has always been a presence in my everyday life. I hope, no, I'm sure, she wouldn't mind that for some years in our household Tehanu was a beloved pet guinea pig, named by my elder daughter. And I like it that a small town on the island of Iffish in the East Reach shares a name with my younger daughter. Whenever my glance falls upon the map of the Archipelago, I smile at that, and meditate on how Ursula's writing has touched so many areas of my life, and how she's been an ever-changing but constant companion through nearly forty years of my different selves.

Tenar and Two Birthdays

VICTORIA MCMANUS

URSULA, you have given me more joy as a reader than I can tell you, and I wish I could offer you more than these few words in return; but perhaps that's fair, and you can make of my words what you will. At least they'll be better than the few words I've managed to stammer on the brief occasions when we've met. This, my gift, is about Tenar, and it's also about me.

I realized I couldn't tell this story well unless I also told you about me. So, in addition to words, I give you a little of myself. It seems only fair, given how much of your self I've had through reading your words.

I can't remember the first time I read the original Earthsea trilogy. I was in elementary school, I suspect, because when I later returned to the books in middle school, they were already familiar companions, and by high school I had started collecting your novels and short story collections. I bought them used, mostly. I had an allowance of $5 a week, and I usually got a trip to the used bookstore once a week as well, where I spent it all on books and comics.

The Tombs of Atuan was and is my favorite of the original trilogy, because it's about a girl, which I guess doesn't surprise you much. My favorite part starts after Ged arrives, because then, all of a sudden, Tenar is the one with the local knowledge Ged needs, and it's thanks to her he can find the Ring of Erreth-Akbe and escape with it. And then, best of all, Tenar gets to leave her isolated, dying desert home behind and go out into the world with Ged, where she can have new adventures. I will admit I was disappointed when she didn't come back in *The Farthest Shore*, and spent years wondering what had happened to her.

On my twenty-third birthday, I read *Tehanu*, while sitting outside in the sunshine, on the grass. I was recently graduated from Bryn Mawr and newly afire with feminist opinions. I was also very depressed that day, because I hadn't gotten into graduate school; and I was working in a dead-end job; and graduation had separated me from the closest friends I'd ever had, all women, and that terrible fact was beginning to sink in; and none of them had called me on my birthday, and I hadn't gotten any cards in the mail. (I did, later.) And on top of all that, I was suffering from a particularly bad month with my Pre-Menstrual Dysphoric Disorder.

You can see how close I feel to you from reading your books, Ursula, because it felt natural to me to expose that fact about myself to you, and I feel you will understand how I must have felt that day.

This is going to sound bad: because I felt so awful, I read *Tehanu*. Maybe this will help: I had been saving it for months, as I often save books by favorite authors.

As I was reading, *Tehanu* was the best book I'd ever read, so good that I almost wanted to cry, or maybe that was because I was feeling sorry for myself, and hormonal, and I felt sorry for Tenar, and…it's difficult to analyze that emotional maelstrom or separate it into components, eighteen years later. Suffice to say, I was consumed by your writing, and your story. I tried to read it slowly, to make it last, but the prose and the story wouldn't let me, even as I was shocked by the horror of what was happening within the story: where was the magic? Where was Tenar's new life I'd always thought she'd have? How could she be a widow, saddled with ungrateful adult children? And how could Therru suffer as she did, in a world that was meant to be a world of hopes and dreams?

But I soon realized I'd been totally wrong about this book. There *was* hope and there *were* dreams. You just had to work for them. You had to *do* things. Nobody handed you magic power on a silver platter; magic was spun from doing dishes and telling stories and keeping goats. When Ged returned to Gont, without magic and without skills, I was sorry, but I understood why; he hadn't earned his magic. Not like Tenar had done. I began to think about this in relation to me, and my life, and it felt like a gift you'd given me directly.

Tehanu was so much better than an Earthsea novel. I felt guilty thinking that at first, almost like a traitor to those books I loved so much as a child, but it is true. It is *so much better*. So much more real. *Tehanu* gave me a new way of thinking about the world, and suddenly my mind was full of new ideas and new connections.

And I realized why the book was so much better to me: you had changed, between writing those first books and this one. *Ursula K. Le Guin*, who at the time was almost a figure of mythical power to me, had changed.

I still remember the force of that revelation. I still feel it. At the time, I knew authors were people. I had met a few professionals, but not as equals. I was a writer, though I didn't really think of myself as a writer in truth. But until then, writers weren't real to me in the way that, suddenly, you had become. You thought one way, and wrote some books. Years later, you felt differently, and wrote another book. Writers aren't static. Books aren't static. And, in sideways fashion, I realized something else this meant: I wasn't always going to be the same writer, either. I could change. Someday, I would be a better writer, a deeper writer, and that growth would never stop.

You gave that to me.

So, Ursula, thank you for Tenar. Thank you for all your books, too, of course, from your short stories to your poems to *Steering the Craft* to your novels to your essays, which remain my favorites in the genre, all your books that have given me uncounted hours of happy reading. Thank you for writing such funny, wacky emails. But most of all, thank you for giving me an example to follow; for showing me what it can mean to be a woman and a writer.

Happy Birthday.

On "On the High Marsh"

JED HARTMAN

BACK IN 2004, I read a Robert Silverberg editorial about what he called the "universal plot skeleton":

> [An] engaging character…faced with some immensely difficult problem that [they must] solve, makes…attempts to overcome that problem,…and eventually…either succeeds…or fails in a dramatically interesting and revelatory way. (*Asimov's* 2004, April/May)

Silverberg essentially claimed that this universal plot underlies all good fiction. There were some interesting discussions online about whether that plot really was universal, and about how to appreciate a work that didn't follow that structure.

A few months later, I read Ursula K. Le Guin's *Tales from Earthsea*, and I particularly liked the story "On the High Marsh."

Because: take Silverberg's universal plot skeleton. Adapt it to an Earthsea-style milieu: perhaps you have a Good Wizard who must go on a Quest to find and stop the Evil Wizard who has devastated the Good Wizard's homeland. In the end, the Good Wizard finds the Evil Wizard, and an epic battle ensues, and the Good Wizard triumphs. Right?

But no. Turn it inside out.

Start with a good wizard (lowercase) who's wandering out in the boondocks. He's maybe a little dim, maybe a little crazy in a gentle sort of way. Look at him through the eyes of a widow with a small farm. She thinks of him as "a silent, damaged creature that needed protection but couldn't ask for it."

The wizard and the widow interact; the wizard does good on various local farms; he has a run-in with a local wizard, in which nobody dies or is even severely injured, though our wizard comes out of it shaken.

And then, right near the end of the story, another wizard comes along, and he tells the widow a story, and the story he tells (summarizes, really) is the Universal Plot Epic Fantasy story outlined above; he's the Good Wizard, and our heretofore semi-protagonist is (or rather was) the Evil Wizard. And when Mr. Good Wizard is done telling the story, he talks with the "evil" wizard, and gently helps bring him back to himself.

No epic battle. The character who would be the protagonist of the epic fantasy — the Good Wizard — doesn't show up until the end of the story, and when he does, he's there to tell stories and heal rather than to fight. The character who is faced with the difficult problem during the course of the story Le Guin is telling doesn't make attempts to overcome the problem, not really; more just trying to cope with everyday life. The Universal Plot is backstory; it's essentially over by the time "On the High Marsh" begins. The other protagonist, the widow, doesn't really have a try/fail cycle here either. (It's not entirely impossible to apply the Universal Plot to this story; it's just that it doesn't apply in remotely the ways that you would expect for a High Fantasy story.)

None of which would matter, except: it works. The story is compelling and sad and moving and rich. It kept me reading, and it kept me caring about the characters, and the ending is completely dramatically satisfying.

Really nicely done. There are other Le Guin stories I like even more, but perhaps none that please me quite so much on structural as well as dramatic grounds.

Tribute to Le Guin/Earthsea

ELLEN KUSHNER

FOR URSULA K. LE GUIN, I betrayed my high school friends. All of them.

And I didn't have that many to begin with. This was in the days before Dungeons & Dragons™ had imparted a modicum of Geek Cool to liking elves and dwarves and wizards. In those days, it was hardcore: fantasy was J. R. R. Tolkien's *The Lord of the Rings* — The Trilogy, all three books of it. No skipping the index, either. We memorized the names of Gondor's kings, and of course learned Elvish Tengwar script so we could pass indecipherable notes in class, and wore grey cloaks made out of bedsheets we dyed in my mom's basement.

I loved the Tolkien, certainly, all three fat volumes of it. But then, one day, a friend gave me a book her mom had brought home from the library, written by her old college friend, "Ussy Kroeber." It was called *A Wizard of Earthsea*.

I read it once. I read it twice. I couldn't believe what was happening to me. This was better than *The Lord of the Rings!!!*

It was about this kid, see, who lived in a world of magic, but he was kind of difficult. He didn't always get along with people, and people didn't always like him. He made bad choices, and he lived with them.

And Earthsea's magic…it was all about words, about language, about speaking, about art. You could memorize lists and spells, but in the end, you were born with power, and you had to learn to use it wisely.

Oh, how I longed to walk the forests of Gont! I longed for them instantly, far more than I had ever for even the most glorious vistas of Middle Earth.

The problem was — what to tell my friends? How could I say to them — "Hey, I found something better than Tolkien!"?

I kept my mouth shut...for awhile. I read everything Le Guin wrote — and I wrote stuff of my own. Oh, I'd been cranking out magical adventures for (and about) my friends and me since I was twelve. But the Earthsea stuff was secret, was mine. It was about a girl who lived in a small house in the woods with a wizard who she wanted for a teacher.... It was intimate, and it was personal. I never finished it — but it set me off in a whole new direction as a writer. I've never looked back.

Sir Walter Scott, the superstar novelist of the nineteentth century who based his work on history and folklore, once wrote that he wrote in "the big bow-wow strain" and wished he could write with "the exquisite touch, which renders ordinary commonplace things and characters interesting..." (1815) like Jane Austen. If Tolkien was the Walter Scott of fantasy, then Le Guin was its Jane Austen. The Earthsea novels of Ursula K. Le Guin taught me that great fantasy doesn't have to be set on sweeping panoramas of lofty towers and heroic battles. Great fantasy can be domestic. It can be about the human struggle to distinguish right from wrong, balance from imbalance, even when it's within ourselves. It can be about who gets the last hot cake, and whose pride is injured, and the need for solitude, and the need for friendship. Le Guin's dragons are all the more grand for living in that world of ordinary things — and my breath still catches when I read of their flight over the sea at dawn. Great fantasy also lets us smell the wind from the fields of Otherwhere, and revel in the fact that it is full of mysteries for us to love. I loved those books so much, that for years I wanted to grow up to be Ursula K. Le Guin. But something strange happened. All that time I spent with her, alone together on the isle of Roke, the courts of Havnor, or out on a boat on the open sea… she taught me to listen to the voice in myself; to heed my own shadow, and draw its lineaments on the page before me, until I could see it perfectly, and name it with words and words and words that would tell its story in many different guises.

Thank you, Ursula. I still love you best.

PREVIOUSLY PUBLISHED IN LIMITED-CIRCULATION EDITIONS (ENGLISH AND FRENCH)

[Untitled]

PAT MURPHY

CONSIDER the remarkable events at Readercon in 1994.

As science-fiction conventions go, Readercon is at the serious and thoughtful end of the spectrum, tending toward serious literary discussions. In 1994, Readercon hosted the James Tiptree Junior Memorial Award, which Karen Joy Fowler and I cofounded back in 1990. Since 1991, the Tiptree Award has been given each year to a work of speculative fiction that explores and expands our view of gender roles.

As part of the planned Readercon program, I interviewed Ursula K. Le Guin. It was a tremendous honor to be asked to interview Ursula. It gave me a wonderful excuse to reread her books and to think what I actually wanted to know about the thoughts and process of a writer I had admired for years.

The interview went well. And after it was done, I somehow — as is so often the case, I can't recall exactly how this came about — ended up on stage with Ursula and a gang of trouble-making feminists in an impromptu and unrehearsed performance of "There's Nothing Like a Dame" from South Pacific. Susan Casper was lead singer, the rest of us (billed, I believe, as Ursula and the Tips) provided backup.

How do these things happen?

I'll bet Ursula knows. Ursula knows a lot — as I learned when I asked her to write fortunes for a set of famous author fortune cookies. (I was making the cookies for a bake sale to support the Tiptree Award, the only serious literary award that is partly supported by bake sales — but that's another story.)

The predictions Ursula gave me were spot on. Who would doubt a fortune that read: "You will find something very odd in the broom closet on Tuesday." I mean, when don't you find something odd in the broom closet (that is, if you happen to have a broom closet)?

Ursula's advice was ever so sage: "Never apologize, never explain, but mumble some of the time." Over the years, I've found that strategy very useful.

Then there is the slightly ominous: "Nothing is following you. Do not look back."

Another fortune struck me as a perfect short story of opportunity missed: "If you eat this before you read it, you will have great fortune." Ah, yes — too late now.

And finally: "You will soon be the Harney County Durum Wheat Queen."

I trust that it will come to pass.

Distant Effects

NANCY KRESS

THE FIRST Le Guin I ever read was *The Left Hand of Darkness*, in 1975, six years after it was first published. The book electrified me.

I had always read SF, but mostly the "Golden Age" authors — Asimov, Sturgeon, Clarke — which was what the local library stocked. After several years of teaching fourth grade in a small town, my life had abruptly changed. Over the course of only two years I married, had a baby, became pregnant with another, and began to write. The stories came out science fiction. They were terrible. All of them earned rejection slips. I had no idea that fandom, SFWA, or conventions even existed. We lived far out in the country and I had no car. I was working in nearly complete isolation.

Then I returned to graduate school, one evening course per semester, in pursuit of the Masters degree that New York State said I must earn to qualify for a return to teaching. My course for fall, 1975 was "Science Fiction as Literature" and one of the texts was *The Left Hand of Darkness*. It amazed me. Immediately I sought out and read *The Dispossessed, The Wind's Twelve Quarters*, and the earlier Rocannon novels.

It would be difficult to overstate the effect these books had on me, particularly *The Dispossessed*. Shevek seemed — and still seems — real and solid and complicated in the way that science-fiction characters simply were not. The prose was simple and eloquent, with the sudden unexpected word or phrase that suggested so much more than it said. When Shevek first connects with Takver during a hiking expedition in the mountains, "Joy was rising mysteriously in him." I read that and thought — yes, that *is* how it feels. Joy both feels mysterious, coming from some other place, and rooted in the body, at one and the same time. Or, in the story "Nine Lives," when Owen Pugh is asked about love and flounders for a reply, he finally comes up with "it's practice, partly." It *is* practice, but a lesser writer would have come up with something more lofty and less pragmatic, which would have been wrong both for Owen Pugh and for truth.

I reread these three books compulsively, and not only for pleasure. On days that my own writing came hard — the babies had kept me up in the night or my story had a Plot Knot or my already crumbling marriage clawed at my mind — I found that reading a few pages of *The Dispossessed* would somehow prime the creative pump. It wasn't that I was imitating Le Guin's writing, or thought I could imitate her. Rather, her assured and graceful prose calmed my mind and centered it, making me eager to return to my own story. I don't know why. Some gifts you just accept.

A decade later, having moved on from the fourth grade, I taught *The Left Hand of Darkness* to college freshmen, along with other SF novels and stories. At the end of the course I asked the students to rank the works we'd studied. The results were interesting. Most of the girls and a few of the brightest boys ranked it first. Most of the boys and the dimmest girls rated it last. Almost no one was in the middle. Winter's hermaphrodites made the eighteen-year-old boys uneasy, and the challenges of the book's structure only appealed to those intelligent enough to see why it mattered.

Twenty years later, in 2008, I held the Picador guest professorship at the University of Leipzig. In my SF course, an innovation for this six-hundred-year-old university in the former East Germany, I taught

The Dispossessed. My students responded with great enthusiasm. They debated the feasibility and desirability of a society without government or money. They offered strong opinions on what Shevek should have done about Sabul's professional blackmail. But when I asked for a show of hands of those who would choose to live on Anarres rather than on Urras, only four hands were raised. East Germany, deprived so long of consumer luxury, wants it now more than it wants anarchistic idealism.

Which would I choose? In 1992 I wrestled with that question as I wrote *Beggars in Spain*. The novella searches for an answer to the question "What do the 'haves' owe the 'have-nots'?" The search terrain lay between two poles, Le Guin's Anarres (everyone is responsible for all) and Ayn Rand's Galt's Gulch (no one owes anybody anything). Neither answer satisfied me, but both led to my best-known work.

Through all these decades of reading and pondering Le Guin, I met her only twice. The first time, Sheila Williams introduced us. Usually I am reasonably poised while meeting people, but this was *Ursula Le Guin*. When I feel flustered and intimidated, I babble. So I did, on and on. I could not stop. The small woman clasping my hand listened, and I saw those intelligent dark eyes grow doubtful that this person was indeed Nancy Kress, or indeed sane. But she was gracious, and eventually I slunk away.

The second meeting went better. At WisCon '96, Ursula and I had a long, lovely conversation about things trivial and profound, including the physiological bases of behavior. At the Tiptree Awards, Ellen Kushner performed a lusty rendition of "Nothing Like a Dame." Nine writers and editors, including Ursula and I, sang back-up. We were collectively terrible. It was fun.

I have not seen her since. But I continue to read her, and now *The Dispossessed* has been replaced as my favorite Le Guin by *Four Ways to Forgiveness*. It's an astonishing quartet of interconnected stories: compassionate without being sentimental, knowing without being self-righteous. Yoss is as solid to me as the computer I am typing this on, and as mysterious. And as joyful.

Usually, the people who greatly influence one's life are people known personally, even daily. But writers are a special class. Like quasars sending out pulses of energy across vast distances, a writer's radiation may affect others far away. Ursula K. Le Guin so affected me. And I am grateful.

A New Island of Stability:
Annals of the Western Shore

JO WALTON

POWERS won this year's Nebula Award for novel. It was a strange choice in some ways — it's fantasy, when the award is more often given to SF; it's the third volume of the Annals of the Western Shore, when few awards are given to later books in series; it's a young adult book, which are traditionally neglected by adult awards; and it hasn't had much fuss made of it up to this point. On the other tentacle, it's a safe choice — nobody could possibly object to giving Le Guin another award, after all, she's probably the most respected genre writer still working. On the third tentacle, the ballot had *Little Brother* and *Brasyl* on it, both SF of the "important" kind that people are talking about. And on the fourth tentacle, *Powers* is such an utterly brilliant book that it entirely deserves the award, indeed it strikes me as the best Nebula winner for some time.

I love this series.

Le Guin wrote a number of wonderful books early in her career, *A Wizard of Earthsea* (1968), *The Left Hand of Darkness* (1969), *The Dispossessed* (1974), and then from *Always Coming Home* (1985) onwards she seemed to become more tentative, questioning what the nature of stories was and what stories it was possible to tell. Her books were never other than interesting, and always beautifully written, but some people said she had like Wells "sold her birthright for a pot of message" and I feel that she was wrestling with questions that were often too apparent, and that this sometimes damaged the fabric of story. It's not that you can't have ideas and messages and questions with too many answers, and you can be as didactic as you like in SF, it's just that you need to have story first, to keep drawing you across. I always felt these books were taking up arms against the unsayable. She was re-imagining her old worlds, revising and re-visioning them from a perspective that was older, wiser, and better informed but lacking the confidence that had created them.

Then, from the stories collected in *The Birthday of the World* (2002) onwards it was as if she found a new island of stability, like the stable elements some people say may lie on the other side of the transuranics. She had found her assurance again. She moved on to new stories. The Annals of the Western Shore, beginning with *Gifts* (2004) and continuing with *Voices* and *Powers*, is marvellous, is major work from a major writer. The concerns — women, slavery, power, and responsibility — are those that have informed much of her work, but here they are fully integrated into the underlying geology of the stories.

The Western Shore is a civilization that was settled out of the great uncrossable desert that lies to the east. It's mostly small city-states of various kinds, with some barbarian nomads out at the edge of the desert. So far, so fairly-standard fantasy world. *Gifts* is set in the far north, among desperately poor people who have strange strong magical powers and practically nothing else. They're scratching out a bare sustenance living from poor land, with very little contact with the rest of the world. Orrec Caspro is supposed to have the power of unmaking — if he points at something with his left hand it should disintegrate. He's heir to his father, who has the power, and used it to win his mother and defend his domain. This book is like a retelling of an old fairytale. I know it isn't, but it has that power of something told and retold, combined with a deeply observed reality of detail. Orrec has to cover his eyes and go blindly about the world to avoid striking anyone by accident, and the details of that blindness and what it means are all fiercely real. It's written in first person from Orrec's point of view, it's a story of growing up, but it's also like a poem, with every word falling in the right place. The people of the uplands are clinging to their magical abilities, conserving them as best they can, turning inwards, when as Orrec realises at last, the whole world is out there, and making is better than unmaking.

Voices is set in the city of Ansul, and is in the first person point of view of Memer Galva, a girl who has oracle powers. Ansul has been captured by Ald, a desert barbarian, and the whole city is enslaved to him, and longing for freedom. *Voices* is the story of how Memer grows up and the city becomes free again, and not in an expected way. Again the physical reality of Ansul is beautifully imagined, and the ritual worship of ancestor shrines and the many gods of the cities is different and effective.

Then in *Powers* we have the story of Gavir, who is a slave. The children growing up in the earlier two books are heirs of domains, and their inherited magic is the magic of those domains. Gavir has magic, the ability to remember things that haven't happened yet, but it has to be hidden. Etra, where he lives, is much like Republican Rome, with slaves kept in much the same way. Ansul, in *Voices*, is also a republic and, in Galvamand where Memer lives, people can choose to become part of the Galva family, though there is a little distinction between those who have chosen and those who were born to it. Here we see a horrible perversion of that, where the Family take in the slaves and prevent them from keeping their own children, and the slaves are considered to have no ancestors of their own. Gavir is being trained to be a tutor-slave, and he grows up with the children of the family and the other slaves, all strongly characterised. Their childhood is in many ways idyllic. There's a siege of the city, they get older, and Gavir's trust and belief in the trust and relationship between the Family and the slaves is violated when his sister dies. He runs away and journeys through many different possibilities before learning who he is, what freedom is, and what he wants.

Powers is, like much SF and fantasy, a coming of age story. It's also an examination of freedom and slavery, of what it means to belong somewhere, of trust and betrayal, of security and choice and responsibility. It has a detailed complex fantasy world. There's often a sense of handwaving about what people actually do all day in fantasy worlds, but there's none of that here, all the details feel exactly right, and Le Guin never mentions a detail that isn't solid. It also fits together in an economic and political way, it feels as if it has real history and a tradition of literature, and it has odd magics always creeping out of corners. In Gavir's experience of life as a slave we get to re-examine Orrec's and Memer's experiences as heirs to their domains and question what they do not question — but we get to do it at our own speed and in the context of wanting to know what happens next. This is a subtle and complex book with a strong thread of story drawing you on through.

THIS PIECE WAS FIRST PUBLISHED ON TOR.COM, 2009

The Exercise of Vital Powers

UNA MCCORMACK

I

"TO BRING BACK the past in memory is a great power. To remember what hasn't yet come to pass is a great power too." So says Gegemer Aytano Sidoy to her nephew, Gavir Aytana Sidoy, the hero of Ursula K. Le Guin's recent novel *Powers*. Gavir has both these gifts, his aunt only the latter — and it is the former she advises him to cultivate: "Hold to the other power, the one your mother Tano had, for it won't drive you crazy." But Gavir — the stolen child, the runaway slave, one of the dispossessed — is desperate to be welcomed, and when that welcome first comes, it is from a man who claims he can teach him to use his other gift. Gavir follows that path, but the visions of freedom it induces — which travel too lightly, which have "no contact with the earth" — almost drive him crazy. Later, carrying a great and precious burden, the girl Melle, Gavir comes to a city of learning where he will be free. "Do you have a good memory?" the poet Orrec Caspro asks him there. "Very good," says Gavir. "That's my power."

Gavir, in the end, chooses his gift for memory over his visionary power. And I find myself pondering this advice, coming as it does from a great visionary, one who has remembered futures such as Anarres, the Valley, Yeowe, and Shindychew. When I read, and reread, *Powers*, I ask myself: how can past memory sustain future remembrance? What can be learned from the special emphasis placed on history by this beautiful and visionary book?

II

Teaching at a university, I often listen to young men and women talk about their ambitions, about their visions of themselves in the years to come. Travel is often mentioned; so is fulfilling work. Happiness is the goal. Gavir too hopes to travel. He hopes to write a book, a grand history of the City States in which he lives. Alongside these ambitions, he also has a future memory of himself: a vague vision of entering a dark room, where a man turns to him and speaks his name. At the start of the book, Gavir does not have the power to interpret this vision; by the time he does, his two ambitions — to learn and to work — will be fulfilled in ways he did not foresee.

Gavir wishes for life, liberty, and happiness. But Gavir is a slave, and whatever he wants depends upon his masters being true to their promise to protect him. They are not. His sister Sallo is murdered by the master's son, who is not punished for the crime. Gavir, leaving the house in which he has been a slave and the Family whom he no longer trusts, is pursued beyond reason by another slave from the house, Hoby, the master's illegitimate son. I have called Gavir the hero of *Powers*, but he is not the kind of hero that has shed blood across history from *The Iliad* onwards. Gavir does not seize liberty by turning upon Hoby and murdering him; he does not use the master's tools to rebuild the master's house. Throughout *Powers*, Gavir commits no acts of violence. He walks. He works. He tells stories. He admits to himself, painfully, all of his illusions about the nature of power; he learns. In time, Gavir comes to the city of Urdile. He enters the darkened room, and the man standing there, Orrec Caspro, turns to him and speaks his name. Urdile is where Gavir can become a free man, citizen, and scholar. He reaches it at the point in his life when he has within himself the power to become all of these things.

This self-knowledge has come by means of a thorough and direct education in the nature of power. Even before Gavir leaves his home in Etra, he has begun to meditate upon the workings of power. The murder of the slave child Miv troubles his assumption that the Father and the Mother will protect him. The sacrifices made by the slaves of Etra during the siege of the city — in Gavir's case, his health, in Sallo's case, her child — are not rewarded. When Sallo is whored and murdered, Gavir is offered blood money, not justice. With his understanding of the world destroyed, Gavir seeks an alternative. In the Heart of the Forest, he thinks that he has found it: a brotherhood of men who value his learning and dream of revolution. But it remains only a dream, and the truth of life amongst the brotherhood is that the same slavery exists there. Here, among the free men, Gavir learns his greatest lesson: that if the women are slaves, none of us is truly free. By the time he comes to the Forest, Gavir already understands the nature of his own slavery. Amongst the Brotherhood, he comes to understand not only the nature of his sister's slavery, but the slavery of Sotur, his first love. He learns how a girl can be free in name but not in fact, and how this arrests the men's dreams of freedom.

Happiness, Aristotle wrote, is "the exercise of vital powers along lines of excellence in a life affording them scope." It is the lives glossed over by that last clause that form the world of *Powers*, the world of the oppressed and the enslaved. *Powers* makes clear to us exactly who enables that affording; upon whose labour the excellence of others rests. And while the world of *Powers* is not ours, we recognize our own in it. In the farm which the Family visits during the summers, memories of which are a source of genuine happiness to Gavir, we can see through the golden haze of nostalgia darker glimpses of our own past: the plantations of the antebellum Deep South, the *latifundia* of Imperial Rome, places where it was "all to the good [...] if the slaves bred up more slaves who knew the work and the land and nothing else, whose whole life was in that dark village by the stream." We can see our present world there too, surely, and the makings of our future world, if we do not intervene.

This is the chain of history which the narrative of *Powers* breaks. By the end of the book, Gavir has fulfilled one of his ambitions. He has travelled — but this has been nothing like the journey that was all he was able to picture in Etra. And although the narrative stops at this point, we have proof of the fulfilment of his other ambition. In our hands we hold his book, his history of the City States. It is not like the other histories of the City States, grand narratives of "kings, senators, generals, valiant soldiers, rich merchants," but something else. It is a history of invisibility; the story of an oppressed man, who, having loved his slavery and trusted his enslavers, was betrayed, and who learned through painful circumstance and painstaking re-evaluation that no man is truly free if any man or woman is unfree. This is the kind of history that Gavir — free man and scholar — will write in Urdile. This is the kind of book that *Powers* is, a book that brings back the past in memory, makes the invisible visible, and re-visions history.

.

III

History without vision is dead end; vision without history is madness. Gavir's first teacher, the educated slave Everra, will not have modern books in his library, and tells him to put his trust in those who are above him. He is tragically wrong. But when he tells Gavir that "in the wilderness you came from, there's nothing for you," he is correct. When Gavir travels to the Marshes, he is surrounded for the first time in his life by people that look like him. He meets the family from which he was stolen: he has an uncle and an aunt. He discovers his whole name — but not even learning his true name grants him access to full powers. Like so many children of diaspora, he returns to the imagined homeland to find it populated by strangers.

In the Heart of the Forest, the women worked and the men dreamt. In the marshes, wisdom is demarcated along with the work: the "sacred medicine" and raw gatherings of the men are set against the cooked food and "foolishness" of women. To remain in the marshes, Gavir would have to become estranged from that part of himself that has hitherto been his chief source of sustenance. His skills of recall and story-making are women's skills. Suppressing them, needing acceptance, he turns to his other gift, and this loss of contact with his history, with the wretched of the earth, nearly drives him insane. The proverb says, "Where there is no vision the people perish." The same holds true of memory.

When I think of a book in which vision has lost touch with history, Cormac MacCarthy's novel *The Road* comes to mind. In this book, the man and the boy travel — like Gavir — but the world through which they pass is one in which the preoccupation with extinction has become all-consuming. It is an exhausted vision; there is no exercise of vital powers.

At the end, the dying man, in a last flight into fantasy, dreams that someone else will come to save his son. The novel collapses into a lamentation for the past. But it is a past to which the book cannot gain access; the lost world is "a thing which could not be put back. Not be made right again." Of course it cannot be put back, put right. But it can still be reordered. History holds the key. It is, as Gavir knows, one of the arts that can bring "some clarity, some hope of meaning, to human emotions and the senseless, cruel record of human wars and governments." The vision is not inevitable. This is the wisdom of "women's foolishness."

IV

Dear Ms Le Guin:

Very soon after opening *Powers* for the first time, I realized that this was a book I had been longing to read for much of my life. It converses with me on subjects that I think about constantly but cannot or will not often discuss; it gives me insight and counsel. And in my mind's eye, I have a memory of an event that never happened and never will: myself at fourteen, reading this book, using it as a guide. This cannot happen; I cannot go to that child and put things back, put them right. But the reading of this book transforms my relationship with her; it remakes my history. I would like to thank you for the quiet true voice that speaks out from the pages of this gift of a book, a book which holds within it the power to remake and to liberate. My best wishes to you for a very happy birthday; my grateful thanks to you for all the gifts of your craft.

[Untitled]

JULIE PHILLIPS

"TO BE WHOLE is to be part: true voyage is return."
— THE DISPOSSESSED

"If you have really had a home, been a homebody, maybe it's easier
to reconstitute one, wherever you are ... You sort of have the home
knack. I never lived anywhere I really felt not at home (except
Moscow, Idaho, and even it had redeeming features)."
— URSULA K. LE GUIN *

Ursula K. Le Guin is an international writer. She has lived in Paris,
London, New York; Cambridge, Massachusetts; Macon, Georgia; the
19th century Russia of Tolstoy; the Antarctica of Scott's journals; the
mythical archives of Lao-Tzu. But she is also a local one. Born in 1929 in
Berkeley, California, she has lived since 1959 in Portland, Oregon. She has
a profound and paradoxical relationship to the West — a set of contradic-
tions she expressed by setting a work of fiction in far-future California
and calling it *Always Coming Home*.

The West she grew up in is a place that can seem, to natives of more
predictable landscapes, fantastic or unreal. It is difficult for an Easterner to

---

* Unless otherwise noted, all quotes are from my interviews and correspondence with
Ursula K. Le Guin, 2007–2010.

imagine having a view of two volcanoes from your living room window — let alone watching one of them explode. Trees as broad as a house, cities built on earthquake faults; how can a Western writer convince an Easterner of this reality? Then, too, most Americans of European descent have lost all sense of themselves as intruders on the landscape. In the California of Ursula's childhood, whites were very aware of themselves as newcomers. Some saw themselves as "settlers," others, including Ursula's own parents, as aliens in a beloved world that did not originally belong to them. Ursula was raised on a threshold, at a liminal site, a frontier.

Ursula's family on her mother's side were pioneers, and she grew up hearing pioneer legends: about the great-uncle who saved himself from a bear by jamming his arm in its mouth, the pistols another uncle gave her grandparents as a wedding present, the bullet hole in the footboard of their marriage bed.[1] Her grandfather, Charles Kracaw, ran a grocery store in the mining town of Telluride, Colorado. Her grandmother, Phebe Johnston, was the sturdy daughter of a Wyoming rancher who named her own daughter after a novel she liked called *Theodora Goes Wild*.

Theodora Kracaw, known as "Krakie," was born in 1897 and raised in Telluride. When the mines closed and the town declined, the family moved to Sacramento and then to Oakland. Krakie studied psychology and economics at the University of California in Berkeley, got her MA in clinical psychology in the summer of 1920, and shortly afterward married law student and World War I veteran Clifton Brown.

Together they had two children, Clifton Jr. in 1921 and Theodore in 1923. But Brown had returned from the war with a persistent lung infection. They moved to Santa Fe for the air; he seemed to be getting better — and then he died suddenly, in the fall of 1923, leaving a twenty-six-year-old widow who later wrote, "It seems to me I got adulthood as another person gets religion — violently and overnight." [2]

She went to live with her mother-in-law in Berkeley, and it was Lena Brown who encouraged Krakie to go back to the university for graduate work. She went to talk to Professor Alfred Kroeber about an anthropology course. A year later, after he returned from field work in Peru, they met again at a party for Margaret Mead.

Alfred Kroeber was then nearly fifty. He was born in 1876, the son of German immigrants, and grew up in New York. His father, Florence Kroeber, had come with his family from Cologne as a child and had built up a thriving business as a designer and importer of clocks and of objets d'art: bronze sculptures, gilded putti, marble Apollos and Aphrodites for formal New York entrance halls. Alfred, the oldest of four close siblings, went to Columbia University, where he was known among his friends as shy, but also mischievous and unconventional.

He seemed destined for a conventional academic career, but while he was studying for his MA in English literature he took a course in American Indian languages from the pioneering anthropologist Franz Boas. Fascinated by the unfamiliar grammatical structures, he took more classes. With Boas as mentor, Alfred did field work in Montana and Wyoming and earned Columbia's first doctorate in anthropology, writing his dissertation on "Decorative Symbolism of the Arapaho."

He moved to California in 1900, and when the University of California set up a department of anthropology a year later, he began teaching there. Photos from this time show a dark-haired, bearded, self-assured man of thirty, posed with his feet firmly planted in the California soil. He went on doing field work, learning as much as remained to learn of the native .

Californian ways of life, studying "the wrecks of cultures, the ruins of languages, the broken or almost-broken continuities and communities, the shards of an infinite diversity."[3] In 1906, he married San Francisco native Henriette Rothschild. She contracted tuberculosis soon afterward and died of it in 1913.

In 1911, Alfred began working with Ishi,[4] the most famous of all his informants. Ishi's tribe, the Yana, had been destroyed by whites, who murdered most of its people and left the rest to starve. Ishi, a man of about fifty, was the sole survivor. He was brought to live in San Francisco, where he worked with Kroeber and others to record everything he knew of the history and culture of his people. Then in 1916 Ishi, too, died of tuberculosis.

Overcome by silent grief, Kroeber spent much of the next ten years in restless wandering. He remained in anthropology but also, for a while, turned to psychoanalysis, being analyzed and then practicing as an analyst. By 1925, when he met Krakie, he was a more contemplative man, his intellectual curiosity joined to a great psychological and spiritual sensitivity. He had an interest in Eastern religion, from the Upanishads to the Tao Te Ching, and loved poetry, especially Goethe, Shelley, and Keats. As a passionate reader and storyteller, he recounted Indian legends to his children, and much of his daughter's early education in myth and fantasy came from his library. Years later, Ursula wrote that if she knew a thing or two about wizards, "perhaps it's because I grew up with one."[5]

Alfred and Krakie, two remarkable people, were brought together by a shared intelligence, thoughtfulness, sense of fantasy, and pleasure in life. As soon as they decided to marry, in early 1926, Alfred bought a house for them on Arch Street in Berkeley. Clif and Ted took their new stepfather's name, and by the end of the year the couple had another son together, Karl. Three years later, on October 21, 1929, St. Ursula's Day, their only daughter was born.

Small, bright, sensitive, and shy, Ursula was the much-loved youngest child of a large, close family. Both her parents had high expectations for their children; they also enjoyed them, liked spending time with them, and were sensitive in helping them with their troubles. Krakie "had the most piercing psychological observation," Ursula recalled. "She could just read a person. And I think my dad was simply kind of wise and experienced and patient." Ursula's great-aunt Betsy Buck, Grandmother Phebe's much younger sister, also lived with the family and took care of the children. There were tensions in the family (Karl was a sickly baby and nearly died; Ted, in adolescence, suffered from depression), but Ursula, the youngest, was relatively sheltered, or else determined to see her family as a shelter. She remembered her childhood as a happy time, and home would always be important to her. Later, when she was writing about lonely travelers and explorers in other worlds, her work would thrive best when she had a family around her.

It was a lively and intellectual household. Alfred and Krakie's circle was large and inclusive, and they often had friends and colleagues to dinner. Le Guin remembered Robert Oppenheimer, then a charismatic physics professor in his thirties, sitting by the fire in her parents' living room, talking: "I think my mother had a crush on him." [6] Many of the Kroebers' academic friends were women, and her parents expected Ursula to study and enter a profession—perhaps, like two of her three brothers, academia.

Other frequent guests were Native Americans who had been Alfred's informants and became his friends. One, Robert Spott, was a Yurok from the Northern California coast, a grave and subtle scholar of his people's history. Another friend, less formidable from Ursula's point of view, was Juan Dolores, a linguist from Arizona's Papago (or Tohono O'odham) tribe. Dolores spent a month every summer at Kishamish, the family's house in the Napa Valley. Ursula remembered him as kind to the Kroeber children, "very brilliant, lovely, and sad."

In the 1930s, Berkeley was full of refugees from Europe, figures Ursula found especially exciting and romantic. The theoretical physicist Shevek of *The Dispossessed* was named after two of those exiles, "a Russian named Sheviakov, charming nut, became a psychologist, and a Pole named Klimek, an anthropologist of some distinction, my first love (I was five, he must have been about 35)." [7]

As she was getting to know different kinds of people, Ursula also absorbed a lot of stories. From her father's library, she took books of Norse mythology, the Norwegian folk tales collected by Asbjørnsen and Moe, the retold Irish folk tales of Padraic Colum, an expurgated children's version of the *Arabian Nights. A Dreamer's Tales*, by Lord Dunsany was important to her because it was not "ancient or ethnological or anony- mous"[8] — it showed her that fantasy worlds could simply be invented. Later, she would draw on this mix of influences she had received from her parents: "Curiosity about people different from one's own kind; interest in artifacts; interest in languages; delight in the idiosyncrasies of various cultures; … a love of strangeness …"[9]

Ursula's brother Karl was her collaborator in stories and storytelling, along with their friend and next-door neighbor Ernst Landauer, the son of a German Jewish family and another refugee. Together they invented a world based on their stuffed toys that was known as the Animal

Kingdom. It was an elaborate realm whose inhabitants staged battles or sent intrepid exploring parties to distant parts of the garden.

"Karl, being the eldest — and a storyteller, too — was probably largely in control; that's probably why there were so many wars," Ursula recalls. "The queen was Karl's doll, Johanna, and the king was Babar, made for me by a friend of my mother's. He was too delicate to play with very much, as Johanna was, so they could sort of stand aside and be king and queen. And the prime minister was Ernst's rabbit, Mookie, who was a pretty sly character. He was a little sort of bent-over furry rabbit, very much a young child's animal, but he had a canny eye. You could tell Mookie knew a lot.

"Among my animals there was a small panda named Austin, after my mother's brother, who was a doctor. And there was a great deal of medicine, and preparing of small bandages, and sewing up little lesions in stuffed-animal hide. I believe that was pretty much my input while Ernst and Karl were planning another battle or revolution." When she was alone, though, Ursula liked to let the imaginary figures explore and have adventures — perhaps prefiguring the ethnographers and exiles who people her science fiction.

She wrote her first completed story at age nine or ten, about "a man persecuted by evil elves. People think he is mad, but the evil elves finally slither in through the keyhole and get him." [10] (Later she added, "I bet I'd been reading Saki." [11]) She read science fiction, too, borrowing or stealing magazines such as *Astounding* from her brother Karl. The intellectual Kroeber children liked to make fun of the magazines' purple prose, but that didn't stop Ursula from submitting a piece of fiction to *Amazing Stories* at age eleven. She felt honored to get a real rejection letter in return.

As a small child, Ursula was extremely shy. She was not disliked, but she was simply too introverted to be friendly to the other children in her class. "I just sat around and watched the other kids play." That made her home and family, her brothers and Ernst and the worlds of her imagination, even more important to her. Ursula's world was the Arch Street house, a safe base from which to explore the inner lands of fantasy.

If the Kroebers were remarkable and imaginative, their house was equally so. It was built in 1907 by the legendary architect Bernard Maybeck, who believed that a well-designed dwelling "will have the same power over the mind as music or poetry."[12] His ambition was not to make his own statement about form, but to explore how the spaces of a house could give pleasure to its inhabitants. His shapes were quirky and organic, his ceilings high, his rooms full of light and shadow.

The Arch Street house, was, Ursula wrote, "nobly proportioned, handsome and generous in material and workmanship, grave, genial, and spacious." The integrity of its design, she came to feel, embodied a kind of morality. For its inhabitants, it made harmony, balance, truth seem within human power to achieve.

Yet to Ursula, the house also had a frightening side. The redwood floors, she wrote, had "a kind of delayed resilience; compressed by a footfall they snap back…after a while…hours, perhaps…. As an adolescent I rather liked to hang over the deep well of the staircase and listen to the invisible people ascending it, or later, to lie in my small room and listen to myself walking around overhead in the attic, the floor repeating every step I had taken there that afternoon."

As a child, however, she found the footsteps terrifying. "I had night terrors for years after seeing *King Kong* at age six, but could handle them pretty well, so long as I knew people were in the house. The first time

I was ever left alone in it, I went into a slow panic. I tried to be brave, but little by little the shadows and the creakings were too much for me. My older brothers were [playing] across the street, and when I leaned from a balcony and wailed aloud, they came at once and were most comforting and remorseful. I wept apologetically, feeling very foolish. Why was I afraid of my own dear house? How could it have become so strange to me?"

There was another house in the family, too, at least as important as Arch Street. In the early 1930s, Alfred and Krakie bought a farmhouse and forty acres of land in the Napa Valley, thenrural and almost inaccessibly remote. The Kroebers named the place Kishamish, after a myth invented by Karl. Like the Arch Street house, it was both a safe space and a "magical" one.

There are not many things that all the Kroeber children agree on, but one of them is that their childhood ended in 1942. America's entry into the Second World War, when Ursula was twelve, broke up the family. The oldest brother, Clif, was twenty-one; after he graduated from the University of California that spring, he enlisted in the navy. Nineteen-year-old Ted joined the Army Air Corps the same year, and seventeen-year-old Karl went into the army in the fall of 1943. At first Alfred too threw himself into the war effort, working long hours as director of a language-training program at Berkeley. Then in the summer of 1943, he had a heart attack. He spent weeks in the hospital, his life hanging in the balance, then long weeks confined to his bed at home. He recovered, but nothing was as it had been.

It was in this atmosphere of worry and loneliness that Ursula entered

Berkeley High School in the fall of 1943. A slight girl with short dark hair and a bookish, romantic temperament, she hated high school. Berkeley High was huge and anonymous, and she felt like "an exile in the Siberia of adolescent social mores."[13] Teenage girls wore bobby-sox and curled their hair, styles that didn't seem to Ursula worth imitating, though she attempted them as a sort of camouflage.

By now she had a best friend, Jean Ainsworth. Sometimes they saved up their money and went riding together in Tilden Park. Sometimes they hung around in the listening booths of a record store they liked on Shattuck Avenue, though they never bought anything. ("We would squeal for Frank Sinatra — with a slight sense of playacting, doing as the other teenagers were doing, but it was kind of fun.") Philip K. Dick worked in the same record store and graduated from Berkeley High the same year as Ursula. But the two writers were both shy and introverted, and they were also separated by class and by the custom that ordained that boys and girls could not be friends. They never met.

And besides, Ursula had stopped reading science fiction. Instead, taking refuge in the Berkeley Public Library, she read the French books because the foreign language section was safely deserted. And she discovered 19th century literature, especially Tolstoy, who became one of her first great loves, the model, for many years, for her fiction. She felt drawn to the seriousness of 19th century fiction. Tolstoy had a sense of drama, a willingness to explore questions of truth and morality, that she had also found in myth and fantasy. Not at home in modernism, feeling no kinship with the critically acclaimed writers of her own time, she looked backward for her inspiration.

During the long summers at Kishamish, with her brothers gone,

Ursula wrote poetry. Later she recalled, "Those summers of solitude and silence, a teenager wandering the wild hills on my own, with no company, 'nothing to do,' were very important to me. I think I started making my soul then." [14]

Ursula had expected to go to the University of California, like her brothers. But Alfred retired in 1946 and, for the 1947–48 school year, accepted a one-year appointment at Harvard. Alfred and Krakie didn't want to leave Ursula alone in Berkeley, and with a Harvard professorship came free tuition. Ursula was told that she would be going to Radcliffe.

One of the first people she met in Cambridge, Marion Ives Willis, recalled Ursula at seventeen as "very shy, very intense, very brilliant." [15] She had a vivid imagination, Willis said, and was thrown into a reverie that winter when, for the first time, she saw snow fall. In public, Radcliffe girls were required to wear skirts (with nylons underneath, held up by garter belts), but Ursula, living at home her first year, evaded the rule and wore jeans on the street. She wore her jeans cuffed and, when nothing else was handy, was known to use the cuffs for an ashtray.

Intellectually, she was idiosyncratic, stubborn, confident to the point of arrogance. Although her parents approved of her plan to become a writer, Alfred in particular felt she should also have another means to earn a living. So she chose to study French, partly with an eye to teaching, and partly because it meant she would not have to study English literature and read writers she didn't want to read. "I was and am extremely balky about that; I feel, it's my art and I get to choose what I put into my head… but you can't take English at Harvard and say sorry Professor, I won't read James Joyce."

Though it would get her in trouble in graduate school, this remained an unshakable principle for Ursula. She later said. "It is extremely important to me to be able to choose what I read, it's part of my being a writer. My daemon or instinct tells me whom to read and when. I obey. When it was a choice between the professors and the daemon the daemon won."

Her years at college required a series of difficult adjustments: to East Coast customs; to the cold; to the atmosphere of intellectual competitiveness and social superiority. There were a number of students at Harvard in the late 1940s who would go on to make their name as writers, including the poets Frank O'Hara, John Ashbery, and Adrienne Rich and the novelists Alison Lurie and John Updike. Ursula knew Rich and Updike slightly: Updike was dating one of her housemates, his future wife, while Rich had broken the heart of one of her friends. (Ursula liked Updike but held Rich's rejection of her friend against her; the two poets were never close.) Other than that, she had very little contact with other writers. After her first year she lived with Willis at Everett House, a "co-op house" for twenty scholarship girls. Within Radcliffe the house seems to have been for Ursula another enclosed, comfortable space, a little like Arch Street had been — a home in a foreign place.

It didn't help that her college career ended badly. In her senior year, she had an affair with a grad student with whom she was deeply in love — until she discovered that she was pregnant. At Christmas, she told him the news, and he responded by breaking up with her. It was her parents, then living in New York, who arranged for her to have an illegal abortion. At first, Ursula felt that not going through with the pregnancy would be evading the consequences of her actions. But Alfred told her that ending it would be "a lesser sin than the crass irresponsibility of sacrificing your training, your talent, and the children you will want to have." [16]

Still, the breakup left her miserable. The summer she graduated, in 1951, to cheer her up, her brother Karl took her on a trip to Europe. Her first sight of the places she'd been reading about not only cheered her up, it inspired her to start work on a novel.

Because she loved the European history she'd absorbed from reading fiction, she decided to write about several generations of a family as they moved around Europe from the 1490s to the early 1900s. The characters in this "completely amateurish and loco" work of fiction, as she later described it, were citizens of a small imaginary country that Ursula called Orsinia.

In keeping with Ursula's academic career, her apprentice work as a writer was almost as far removed as it was possible to get from literary trends and contemporary subject matter. A writer who has been formed by, among others, Native American myth, the Tao, and Tolstoy is stuck with a diverse and seemingly irreconcilable set of influences. Nor did she feel she could speak for her contemporaries at Harvard; nor did a woman writing in the 1950s have many models for her fiction. "I didn't know who my fellow writers were," she later said. "There didn't seem to be anybody doing what I wanted to do."

Instead, borrowing from the 19th-century realists she loved, she invented a nonexistent Eastern European country where she could set fiction of her own design. Its name, Orsinia, was a sly pun on her own name's ursine connotations. "Since most of what I knew came out of books," she said, "I made up a place that was like the places in books I liked to read. But as soon as I began to work in Orsinia, I realized I didn't have to imitate Tolstoy. I had created a place I could write about in my own terms."[17] She eventually wrote at least one novel and a number of short stories set in Orsinia; it was the place where she began to find her voice as a writer.

Her parents followed these early writing attempts with interest. "I generally showed things to them until I wasn't living with them anymore, and even then I'd send them things.

"My mother could be a fairly stern critic, or at least questioner ('What is this book about?' — that was an early draft of *Malafrena*). [But] I think they both came to believe that I had talent and was right in pursuing it."

In the fall of 1951, Ursula started graduate school in French at Columbia. The first year she lived with her parents on Riverside Drive; Karl, who was studying literature at Columbia, was also nearby. The second year, Alfred and Krakie went back to Berkeley. Ursula moved into a graduate women's dorm, while Karl, she recalled, had a little apartment on 126th Street "that smelled deeply, deeply of cats. It was a kind of strange year for me, a bit lonesome and pinched for money."

The topic she chose for her PHD thesis was the 16th-century poet Jean Lemaire de Belges. She later said she wrote about him "because nobody else loved him." As a subject, he seems a bit like the foreign language section of the Berkeley library: a room with no other readers. But Ursula also saw him as a transitional figure: his poetry, though mostly conventional, shows hints of a Renaissance he wasn't in the right time or place to enjoy. He couldn't see the currents of his time, she later observed, and had no idea where he was going. "I think as a young writer I felt some sympathy there, because I was going in another direction than the critically approved culture."

Meanwhile, studying French felt less like the right thing to do. As Ursula approached her preliminary exams, she began to resist. She didn't care for the French Existentialists, who were "too sour and aloof" for her taste. She refused to read André Gide, who was required for her exams. She had never really been at home in "formal Lit Crit," she later wrote, "even when I could turn off a term-paper on obscure 16th-century French poets with a flick of the wrist." [18] She had been in school too long, and she had reached the uncomfortable point of having gone as far as she could in French and found nothing for her there.

Then, at twenty-three, she got a Fulbright scholarship to study for a year in France. And France changed everything.

In the fall of 1953, the Fulbright scholars bound for Paris all went over together in a long, austere, and endlessly exciting voyage on the Queen Mary. At the end of the first evening's dinner, at a long table full of graduate students, Ursula asked if anyone would like to go to the steerage bar for a liqueur. From the other end of the table, she recalled, "one sole soft voice responded in a seductive Southern accent: 'yayus.'"

The voice belonged to a young historian named Charles LeGuin, a tall, handsome Georgian with a flattop who was studying at Emory University in Atlanta. They talked, and talked some more, and by the time the boat docked at Le Havre, Ursula had fallen in love. It took some time for Charles to propose, she recalled: "ten days or so. I thought he never would."

They were sent to stay in the Paris suburbs, but quickly got permission, along with two friends, to move into a hotel in the Quartier Latin. Ursula shared a third floor room; Charles was on the fifth. Though the accommodations were austere and the facilities primitive — "the toilet paper was usually the Copenhagen *Morgenblatter*, which seemed appropriate" —

the four friends were deeply happy. Ursula and Charles announced their marriage plans to Ursula's parents, who gave their blessing sight unseen: "Alfred and Krakie were both pretty intuitive, and I guess they could read the truth and happiness in my letters." Even the Fulbright commission were happy to help—in Ursula's recollection, they were pleased the young couple weren't in worse trouble.

But the paperwork required by the French government took all fall to assemble. Ursula recalled, "We can both still see the look of grim defeat on the face of the [official] at the Bureau of Marriages or whatever it was when at last we put all our documents with all their tax stamps in all the right places, and the Ambassador's signature, under her iron wicket; and then the slow, faint, dawning frown of bliss as she went through them all again, and looked up at last, and said, 'But *monsieurmademoiselle*, these papers are unacceptable, your name is misspelled throughout.'

"Charles's family spelled the named all in one, LeGuin. As the iron lady almost cheerily explained, it could be Leguin, or it could be Le Guin, but it could under no circumstances be LeGuin. She had not previously pointed this out, but you do not argue through those wickets. We had one day left before our banns expired (they had to be posted in the Mairie du Sixième Arrondissement, where we were to be married, for three weeks previous to the marriage). We took taxis all that day to every office in Paris, got the spelling changed, initialed, and tax-stamped at each one, and brought the documents back to the iron lady. She looked them all over very slowly, and finally pushed them back under the wicket with a smile—a thin, grim, pinched smile, but all the same, in the circumstances, heroic. *'Je vous félicite,'* she said." Congratulations.

On December 22, 1953, the winter solstice, they married in the Mairie.

Then, finally, they moved together into a shabby room of their own.

Paris in 1953 was, like the rest of Europe, still rebuilding from the war. The French women dressed chicly but soberly, Ursula recalled, and even the food was spartan. "But all the theaters were open, and we went to all the plays and operas and ballets and concerts for practically nothing; and the bookstalls on the Seine actually sold interesting second-hand books and prints; ...and tourism was almost nonexistent, so the streets were ours, and if we went to Versailles or the Louvre or Notre-Dame we could wander alone as we pleased and not be herded about in droves. And maybe because the winter was so long and dark, April in Paris was all it should be. Our Paris wasn't very glamorous but it was intensely endearing. I wouldn't trade it for anybody else's."

Charles was hard at work, but Ursula let her research gently slide. "I went to the Bibliothèque Nationale with Charles sometimes, and fiddled around with Jean Lemaire. I loved handling the old books, and the language and all. But I wasn't serious. Charles was doing real research and building up his thesis. I had got free. I was writing short stories and a novel. We were each doing what we most wanted to do."

Ursula didn't "reinvent herself" in Paris; stubborn and self-assured, very much her own person, she was not one to cast off old selves or acquire new ones. But she cast Jean Lemaire de Belges back into obscurity, to await the compassion of future grad students; and with marriage to Charles giving her the beginnings of a family of her own, she devoted herself to writing poetry and fiction.

In the summer of 1954, the Le Guins returned to the United States. They went out to California to see Ursula's family, then took the train to

Macon, Georgia, Charles's hometown. Charles got a job teaching history at Mercer University in Macon, and Ursula was hired as an instructor in French.

Georgia was a new world for the "Yankee" Ursula, "more foreign to me in some ways than France." (Even being called "Yankee" was strange to her until she realized that it was simply the name for "someone who doesn't know anything about the South and is patronizing.") She recalled a neighbor "who asked me kindly, when I was waiting for the bus in front of her house with Charles, 'And how do you like this country, dear?' I think she thought I was French." She also recalled her bafflement at the sign in the Atlanta train station that said "Colored Drinking Fountain," and her horror when she realized what it meant. It was, she said, "one of the few times I have felt the sensation of the 'blood running cold.'"

But she loved Charles's family. Charles's father was a railroad clerk, and Charles was the first in his family to go to college. Ursula, the daughter of academics from California, "was a real problem to them in some ways, because I was so different. But his people were open-hearted and non-judgmental." It was a large, warm extended family: Tom and Ella Peavy LeGuin "both had eight siblings, and most all the uncles aunts and cousins lived within twenty or thirty miles of Macon.... There was an awful lot of visiting and iced tea and hearing about did y'all hear about Gracie Mae's tumor the size of a cantaloupe, but it was seldom entirely uninteresting."

Meanwhile, Ursula went on writing and trying to get published. In 1955, the twenty-four-year-old author submitted the manuscript of her Orsinian novel *The Necessary Passion* (later renamed *Malafrena*) to an old friend of her father's, the publisher Alfred Knopf. In July she reported to her parents that Knopf himself had returned the manuscript, along

with a letter saying that the climate wasn't quite right for this sort of fiction, but encouraging her to submit other work. The kind words, she said,
were "all the impetus I needed to keep going."

For a little while, Alfred acted as Ursula's poetry agent, searching out
literary journals and submitting her work. "He discovered that the little
magazines are, as he put it, an interesting subculture. He certainly placed
several poems, and we mutually rejoiced. It was a lovely thing of him to
do.... He was, after all, busy, actively writing himself, right up to the end
of his life."

The year in Macon was followed by one in Atlanta, where Charles
taught at Emory and Ursula worked as secretary to the physics department. That spring, Charles, his dissertation done, got two job offers, one
from the University of Virginia and one from the University of Idaho.
The Virginia job was a good one, and they both would have liked to stay
close to Charles's home and family. In the end, it was segregation that
sent them out of the South. After Charles came back from his interview
with the "hidebound" university of Virginia, Ursula recalled, they talked,
"and what it came down to was, 'I don't want to bring up children here.'"

Instead, in the summer of 1956, the Le Guins moved to Moscow, Idaho,
where in July 1957 their daughter Elisabeth was born. In 1959, they went
on to Portland, Oregon, and its new urban university, Portland State. In
November of that year the second of their three children, Caroline, was
born, and a few months later they bought the house with a view of two
volcanoes.

From the beginning, when Elisabeth came home from the hospital
and Ursula, struggling to put a diaper on her straight, relinquished the
job to the more talented Charles, the two parents cared for their children

together. Charles "undertook fatherhood in the most matter-of-fact way as a completely shared responsibility," Ursula recalled, and that made all the difference to her writing. "He was out of the house all day working, but I could rely on him: when he was here, he was here." She was part of a family again, and that feeling of being in a family would give her, over the years, a security that allowed her to send her characters out to explore.

In September 1960, Alfred and Krakie flew to Europe for a conference in Austria, then went on to Paris. There, late in the evening of October 4, Alfred said he couldn't get his breath. He died that night of heart failure at the age of eighty-four. Ursula, at home in Portland, first heard of his death on the morning radio news.

Krakie, a widow again at sixty-three, went on with her work and life. A year later she finished what would be her best-known book, *Ishi in Two Worlds*, and nine years later she married a man more than forty years younger than she. But the hole Alfred left in all their lives was a large one. Ursula turned thirty-one a few weeks after her father's death, and later said it was that year she finally felt she had "come of age."

In the summer of that next year, 1961, Ursula's first published story appeared in the *Western Humanities Review*. "An die Musik," its title taken from Schubert's ode to the power of music, is a story about a poor composer who — very much like his creator — is determined to go on writing despite his family obligations and his lack of recognition. This slippery story begins as an exploration of Rilke's question "Must I write?," then evades the dilemma, shifting to a consideration of music's ethical implications in general. Ursula, however, had clearly already answered the question for herself.

In the end, Orsinia was not the right home for her imagination. It had been a comfortable private space for her, but an isolated one. Even the characters in her Orsinian stories are often trapped in situations from which they long to escape. When she sent the stories to publishers, she got them back with rejection slips saying, "This material seems remote." It was intended to be remote, but it was too much so. It was more consciously sophisticated than her later science fiction and fantasy but lacked its wildness, its surprises, its pure electrifying energy. She was not yet writing on the frontier.

Not long after the Le Guins came to Portland, a friend loaned Ursula some science fiction magazines. Her next published story appeared in the magazine *Fantastic* in September 1962. "April in Paris" is a fantasy about a struggling young academic who gives up all his book learning and steps instead into the world opened to him, one rainy night in his garret, by a successful act of magic.

NOTES:

1   Of the bullet hole Le Guin says, "The story I know is that they were lying in bed (long before they were grandpa and grandma) in Wyoming or Colorado or somewhere and she had her pearl-handled revolver under the pillow and he was teasing her, 'You couldn't hit my big toe from here with that little thing!' And she got mad and did — nearly.

    "The angle of entry of the bullet, however, puts this fine story in much doubt. For other versions, you would have to ask my brothers. I think you would get three entirely other versions."

2   Kroeber, Theodora, *Alfred Kroeber: A Personal Configuration* (1970). Berkeley: University of California Press, 1979, p. 130.

3 Le Guin, Ursula K., "On the Frontier," in *The Wave in the Mind: Talks and Essays on the Writer, the Reader, and the Imagination*. Boston: Shambhala, 2004, p. 29.

4 The Yana, like the people of Earthsea, did not tell their true names to others. "Ishi" meant simply "man."

5 Le Guin, Ursula K., to Eleanor Cameron, April 27, 1970. Division of Special Collections & University Archives, University of Oregon.

6 Le Guin, Ursula K., to Virginia Kidd, Oct. 12, 1970. Courtesy Virginia Kidd Agency.

7 Le Guin, Ursula K., to Darko Suvin, October 19, 1974. Division of Special Collections & University Archives, University of Oregon. The two men were George V. Sheviakov and Stanislaw Klimek, an anthropologist from the University of Lvov who worked with Alfred Kroeber at Berkeley for a couple of years in the 1930s and who, according to Ursula, was killed in the Second World War.

8 Le Guin, Ursula K., review (2004) of Lord Dunsany, *In the Land of Time and Other Fantasy Tales*, edited by S. T. Joshi. *http://www.ursulakleguin.com/UKL-Review-Joshi-LordDunsany.html*. Accessed 2010.

9 Le Guin, Ursula K., to Eleanor Cameron, October 2, 1969. Division of Special Collections & University Archives, University of Oregon.

10 Le Guin, Ursula K., "A Citizen of Mondath" (1973), in Le Guin, *The Language of the Night: Essays on Fantasy and Science Fiction*. New York: HarperCollins, 1992, p. 21.

11 Goldsmith, Francesca, "Ursula Major." *School Library Journal* vol. 50 no. 6, June 1, 2004, p. 52.

12 Ursula K. Le Guin, "Living in a Work of Art." *Paradoxa* no. 21, 2008, pp. 122–135. The quotations that follow, through "…strange to me," come from the same article. The building, known as the Albert Schneider House after its first owner, stayed in the Kroeber family until Krakie's death in 1979.

13 Le Guin, Ursula K., "My Libraries" (1997), in *The Wave in the Mind: Talks and Essays on the Writer, the Reader, and the Imagination*. Boston: Shambhala, 2004, p. 21.

14 Le Guin, Ursula K., in Connie C. Rockman, ed., *The Ninth Book of Junior Authors*. New York: H. W. Wilson, 2005, p. 310.

15 Interview with Julie Phillips, June 2007.

16 Le Guin, Ursula K., "The Princess" (1982), in Le Guin, *Dancing at the Edge of the World*. New York: Harper & Row, 1989.

17 Le Guin, quoted in Elizabeth Cummins, *Understanding Ursula K. Le Guin*, pp. 128–29. Columbia, South Carolina: University of South Carolina Press, 1993.

18 Le Guin, Ursula K., to James Tiptree, Jr., January 8, 1973, in "Dear Starbear: Letters Between Ursula K. Le Guin and James Tiptree, Jr." *The Magazine of Fantasy & Science Fiction*, September 2006, pp. 87–88.

Ulysses Kingfisher

PATRICK O'LEARY

THERE ONCE was a Ulysses
who turned into a Mrs.
leaving untold riches
for the hearty.

There's no way to show her
the honor to know her —
Can't someone just throw her
a party?

Seven Ways of Looking at Ursula K. Le Guin

ELEANOR ARNASON

I HAVE BEEN TRYING to imagine what American science fiction would be like without Ursula K. Le Guin. When biologists want to find out what a gene really does, they remove it from mice — the mice are called "knock-out" mice — and then see what happens. This is not a nice thing to do to the mice, but it is often informative.

I am doing a thought experiment version of this. For example, imagine what science fiction would be like without H. G. Wells, whose short novels have cast a long shadow over the field. What would we be without *The Time Machine*, *War of the Worlds*, and *The Island of Dr. Moreau*?

Where would we be without Ursula K. Le Guin?

I can see six areas where the field would be diminished.

One is feminist science fiction. Le Guin is certainly not the only fine writer of science fiction about women and their issues. Joanna Russ and Suzy McKee Charnas come to mind, among many others. But Le Guin has written often and deeply about gender roles, beginning with *The Left Hand of Darkness* in 1969, which was pretty darn early, about the time the Second Wave of Feminism hit me. (I spent six months or maybe an entire year continuously angry after the wave rolled over me in 1968 or 9. Since I had been raised by feminists, it should not have hit so hard; but it did.) This was about the same time *Star Trek* began bringing lots of women into the science-fiction community. Le Guin was there at the start and has stayed with feminism for the forty years since then.

I can't talk about the early days of feminism in the sf community, because I was off by myself in Detroit, having lost touch with fandom, though I was reading and writing. I can't remember the first time I read *The Left Hand of Darkness*, but I know it was soon after the novel was published. It had a huge impact on me. A beautiful novel, though I don't think Le Guin should have killed Estraven. I have reread it many times.

The second area where science fiction would be diminished without Le Guin is anthropological science fiction. She isn't the only person or the first person to write this kind of sf, but she has done it beautifully and intelligently. My favorite novel by her may be *Always Coming Home*, which reads like an anthropological text, except for one small narrative thread, the story of Stone Telling Woman. I prefer the anthropological parts of the novel: the folk tales, plays, descriptions of how villages are laid out, and the recipes. The meat[1] of the novel, what's really important about it, is this information. It shows — as does Italo Calvino's *Invisible Cities* — that a novel does not need to be a ninteenth century narrative about richly interiorized characters. That is only one alternative among many.

Le Guin can create wonderful characters, but she knows that there is more to life than psychology, and it's possible to make a novel out of landscape or cityscape or details.

Science fiction has suffered often from the pulp action plot and sometimes from a belief in psychology and character development. Le Guin shows us neither is necessary: a valuable lesson.

As an aside, I go through copies of *Always Coming Home*, because they sit in the kitchen with my cookbooks and get bent and stained and have to be replaced. I like one of the recipes a lot.

The third area where Le Guin matters is anarchism; and here she does not share the stage with a lot of other science fiction writers. The only other contemporary anarchist writer I know is the Mexican historian and novelist Paco Ignacio Taibo II. In his crime novel *An Easy Thing*, the private eye hero is hired to find out how Emiliano Zapata really died *and* who killed the Mexican Revolution. A terrific book, though more like Raymond Chandler than Le Guin.

The Dispossessed is Le Guin's famous anarchist novel, another book I have read many times. It's also a utopian novel, though an ambiguous one. But most of human life is ambiguous to some extent.

A respect for self-action and self-realization runs through her work. Here is a quote from "Dancing to Ganam," a story published in 1993:

> Ganam is one little city-state on a large planet, which the Gaman called Anam, and the people in the next valley call something else entirely. We've seen one tiny corner of it. It'll take us years to know anything about it. Dalzul, because he's crazy or because churtening made him crazy or made us all crazy, I don't know which, I don't care just now — Dalzul barged in and got mixed up in sacred stuff and maybe is causing trouble and confusion. But these people *live* here. This is their place. One man can't destroy them and one man can't save them! They have their own story, and *they*'re telling it!

The key words are: "They have their own story, and *they*'re telling it!" Le Guin says this often. It's something that anthropologists — real ones on our planet — need to remember. The people they study are living in their home place and telling their own story. A lot of anthropology, especially in the second half of the twentieth century, has been learning how scholars have patronized the people they studied and misunderstood what they were seeing or being told.

I am not an expert in anarchism, in spite of a fondness for the IWW. But I know it's about self-determination and a belief that Hobbes was wrong: human life is not naturally nasty, brutish, and short. People do not need a repressive government in order to behave decently.

In "Dancing to Ganam" and many other places, Le Guin argues that people know their own lives better than anyone else. Only they have the knowledge necessary to make good decisions. No matter how wise and kind a government or a hero may be, it or he or she does not know enough. That's what kills Dalzul: ignorance and arrogance. He has walked into someone else's story and thinks he knows what is going on.

This brings me to Taoism, another area where Le Guin is important. As with anarchism, she does not share this area with many other science fiction writers. There is plenty of science fiction that is suspicious of experts and know-it-alls, as well as a lot of sf that admires super-competent heroes. But most sf writers who are wary of super-competence do not root their wariness in the *Chuang Tzu* and *Tao Te Ching*.

I am going to fold Taoism in with anarchism, because they look similar to me.

There is something anarchistic about this quote:

> Exterminate the sage, discard the wise,
> And the people will benefit a hundred fold.
> Exterminate benevolence, discard rectitude,
> And the people will again be filial.

> Exterminate ingenuity, discard profit,
> And there will be no more thieves and bandits.[2]

And about this quote:

> If we stop looking for "persons of moral superiority" to put in
> power, there will be no more jealousies among the people. If we
> cease to set store by products that are hard to get, there will be no
> more thieves.[3]

It is futile, the Taoists seem to argue, to try and solve social problems
by putting wise men or good men or heroic men in power. Discrimination
and hierarchy are what cause trouble in the world. If we have heroes, we
have the un-heroic. If we have sages, we have fools. The rich create thieves.
Rulers create the subservient and the insubordinate.

Or as *The Internationale* puts it:

> We want no condescending saviors
> To rule us from their judgment hall.
> We workers ask not for their favors.
> Let us consult for all.
> To make the thief disgorge his booty.
> To free the spirit from its cell.
> We must ourselves decide our duty.
> We must decide and do it well.[4]

According to the historian Joseph Needham, Taoism performed a holding action for the Chinese people over the many centuries until socialism appeared.[5]

There is something else that Taoism may share with anarchism: a distrust of abstraction, a liking for the concrete and specific. "The (true) sage is for the belly, not the eye,"[6] the Tao Te Ching says.

A more elitist passage says: "Therefore in governing the people, the (true) sage empties their minds, but fills their bellies."[7]

T-Bone Slim says:

> I pray dear Lord for Jesus' sake
> Give us this day a T-Bone steak.
> Hallowed be Thy Holy name,
> But don't forget to send the same.
>
> Oh, hear my humble cry, O Lord,
> And send us down some decent board,
> Brown gravy and some German fried,
> With sliced tomatoes on the side…
>
> Oh, hear me, Lord, I'm praying still,
> But if you won't, our union will
> Put pork chops on the bill of fare
> And starve no workers anywhere.[8]

There's a lot of food in the iww songbook, right through to "pie in the sky bye and bye" on the last page.

I'm at the edge of my area of competence here, so will go back to Le Guin and her love of the concrete and specific. This is from "Dancing to Ganam":

> He listened as he walked in the streets of Ganam. He tried to look, to see with his eyes, to feel, to be in his own skin in this world, in this world, itself. Not his world, not Dalzul's, or Forest's or Riel's, but this world as it was in its recalcitrant and irreducible earth and clay and stone, its dry bright air, its breathing bodies and thinking minds. A vendor was calling wares in a brief musical phrase, five beats, tataBANaba, and an equal pause, and the call again, sweet and endless. A woman passed him and Shan saw her, saw her absolutely for a moment: short, with muscular arms and legs, a preoccupied look on her wide face with its thousand tiny wrinkles etched by the sun on the pottery smoothness of the skin. She strode past him, purposeful, not noticing him, and was gone. She left behind an irreducible sense of being. Of being herself.

There are some very typical Le Guin words here: recalcitrant, irreducible. Reality for her is solid, specific, stubborn, impossible to reduce, like T-Bone Slim's pork chops and the *Tao Te Ching*'s filled bellies.

There is another contribution that Le Guin has made to science fiction, and I'm surprised I've gotten this far without mentioning it. She writes about aging. Science fiction tends to have young heroes or thousand-year-old heroes in young bodies. For those of us who creak in the morning and see mortality on the horizon, it's nice to have heroes like Odo in "The Day Before the Revolution."

I have difficulty with her descriptions of the aging Ged, who no longer has the power he once did, maybe because — like so many Americans — aging is scary for me. Gandalf is more reassuring. So are the Taoist sages with their long, white beards and their magic, seated comfortably on flying cranes.

But as long as we have aging and death, we need to deal with these issues in our fiction. Too few science fiction writers do this.

Finally, Le Guin is an intelligent, elegant, beautiful writer in a field that is not full of great stylists. Listen to this from "A Fisherman of the Inland Sea":

> Then I would go up to my room under the eaves, my room of dark wood walls and dark red curtains, the smell of rain coming in the window, the sound of rain on the tiles of the roof. I would lie there in the mild darkness and luxuriate in sorrow, in great, aching, sweet, youthful sorrow for this ancient home I was going to leave, to lose forever, to sail away from on the dark river of time. For I knew, from my eighteenth birthday on, that I would leave Udan, leave O, and go out to the other worlds.

She has more guts than I do. I wouldn't use "dark" four times in a paragraph. But it works.

So, Le Guin is a feminist writer; a writer of anthropological science fiction; a writer suspicious of great men, even though she created Shevek, who is a genius; a writer in love with tangible reality and everyday experience: songs, folktales, gardens, recipes, city streets, the kind of things that anthropologists describe.

Her reality is usually one of spare landscapes — ice sheets, deserts, and oceans — or human landscapes, towns and houses. She writes lovely towns. The one exception I can think of is *Always Coming Home*, set in her native landscape of Northern California. That novel is more densely biological, its nature more detailed, than is most of her fiction.

Maybe we should go to the root of "anthropological." Le Guin writes about people, especially about humans. The non-humans she has described most closely — her dragons — turn out to be humans, sort of.

This is what we would have lost, if accident or some scientist with extraordinary power had knocked Le Guin out of science fiction.

PERSONAL NOTE:

A seventh kind of diminishing occurs to me, not a lessening of the field in general, but of my own writing.

Years ago David Lenander asked me to describe what Le Guin has meant to me personally as a writer. It was on a panel at a convention; and Le Guin was in the audience. I said it was like asking a fish about water. Le Guin's writing has been my environment. I would probably have become a writer without her. I knew from early childhood that I wanted to tell stories. But I have no idea what kind of writer I would have been in her absence.

NOTES:

1   I don't know why I write meat. I'm not crazy about meat. Maybe I mean "the rice of the novel, its pasta or beans or spaghetti squash…"

2   Chapter 19 of the *Tao Te Ching*, translation by D.C. Lau (Penguin Books, 1963).

3 Chapter 3 of the *Tao Te Ching*, translation by Arthur Waley (Wordsworth Editions, 1997).

4 *Songs of the Workers To Fan the Flames of Discontent* (the IWW Songbook), 1974 edition.

5 This is from Needham's discussion of Taoism in his *Science and Civilization in China* (Cambridge University Press series). I don't have a specific quote.

6 *Tao Te Ching*, Chapter 12, Lau translation.

7 *Tao Te Ching*, Chapter 3, Lau translation. Remember this book is more than two thousand years old. It can be elitist as well as anti-elitist.

8 IWW Songbook.

Ursula K. Le Guin's Narratives of Healing

DEIRDRE BYRNE

FOR URSULA K. LE GUIN, narrative is a fundamental function of language and of human being. She writes in her essay, "Some Thoughts on Narrative":

> Narrative is a stratagem of mortality. It is a means, a way of living. It does not seek immortality; it does not seek to triumph over or to escape from time (as lyric poetry does). It asserts, affirms, participates in directional time, time experienced, time as meaningful....
>
> To put it another way: Narrative is a central function of language. Not, in origin, an artefact of culture, an art, but a fundamental operation of the normal mind functioning in society. To learn to speak is to learn to tell a story. (1989, 39)

This overarching view of narrative is a far cry from the dominant empiricist epistemology of modernism, in which the referential function of language is privileged over the imaginative: words are used to point to things, ideas or phenomena, not to tell stories. In this article, I will explore Le Guin's use of narrative as a means of constructing identities and as a process of healing for individuals and societies. In some of the texts I examine here, Le Guin tells stories of the way an individual achieves healing; in others, she uses the narrative process itself to bring about wholeness.

Autobiography, telling the story of one's life, is also called "life writing." Narrative therapists call it a "self-story" (Payne 2006, 16, 17). They emphasize that the goal of narrative therapy is to arrive at a story with "unique outcomes and preferred developments" (Freedman 1996, 132): that is, preferred by the subject of the narrative. A narrative of this kind tells how the person is enabled to create a better "ending" than the position s/he began in. Le Guin's "A Woman's Liberation" (collected in *Four Ways to Forgiveness* [1995]), in which Radosse Rakam narrates her own liberating journey from slavery on the planet Werel to educational activist on Yeowe, is one such tale.

Rakam opens her self-story with the words:

> *My dear friend has asked me to write the story of my life,* thinking it might be of interest to people of other worlds and times. I am an ordinary woman, but I have lived in years of mighty changes and have been advantaged to know with my very flesh the nature of servitude and the nature of freedom. (Le Guin 1995, 195, italics in original)

Rakam's life story begins with a position of extreme disempowerment: she is born into a slave family on Werel, where she is known as an "asset" (Le Guin 1995, 196). The word marks her position in an economic system where people are owned and used in exactly the same way as tools or appliances. Rakam is repeatedly traumatized as a result, and her narrative recounts how she crafts an identity and achieves wholeness through personal, sexual, and political empowerment. Her tale has affinities with Jerome Bruner's essay on "The Narrative Creation of Self," where he argues that to recount events, to tell the story of what happened to one, is to construct an identity:

> The construction of selfhood, it seems, cannot proceed without a capacity to narrate.
>
> Once we are equipped with that capacity, we can produce a selfhood that joins us with others, that permits us to hark back selectively to our past while shaping ourselves for the possibilities of an imagined future. (2004, 13)

Indeed, as Rakam explores her subservient past on Werel through her narrative, and recounts the steps she took to overcome her disempowerment, she asserts the value of the identity she has created for herself and looks forward to a meaningful future. Rakam's story narrates how she overcomes several obstacles to her own empowerment, including illiteracy, destitution, and complete legal dispossession. In the process of telling the tale, she constructs a more desirable self, within the context of Yeowan culture and society.

A comparison with the companion story, "A Man of the People," which immediately precedes "A Woman's Liberation," reveals that Havzhiva, the subject of that story, is not subjected to sexual abuse as Rakam is, although in many other respects his self-story follows a similar trajectory from imprisonment by customary ideas within his community to educational and political freedom. Indeed, Havzhiva's narrative is much less dramatic than Rakam's, partly because his liberation is not sexual, but educational. This is no coincidence, since Rakam's trauma as an "asset" on Werel includes sexual domination or "use" by anyone who has more property than she does. When her sexuality is violated by rape, her personal agency is removed, and her liberation crucially involves learning how to choose encounters that suit her body and her well-being. Being more thoroughly and intimately oppressed than Havzhiva, and therefore more traumatized, means that Rakam has a longer journey to personal freedom than he does.

Rakam writes that, as an asset of the Shomeke family, she could be "used" for sexual purposes by men or women at any time:

> Perhaps you will say that I could not or should not have had pleasure in being used without my consent by my mistress, and if I did, I should not speak of it, showing even so little good in so great an evil. But I knew nothing of consent or refusal. Those are freedom words. (1995, 205–6)

These comments on her own availability to be "used" sexually link crucial themes in Rakam's narrative: personal and sexual agency is intermeshed with economic freedom. In other words, there is no difference between the freedom to dispose of one's own body at will, and legal or financial freedom. Only those who are not slaves, but free, have the psychological power of consent and refusal. When Rakam leaves the Shomekes' estate and travels to the free planet of Yeowe, where slavery has ended in "Liberation" three years previously, she is surprised to be put to work farming rice in a co-operative plantation. Here she discovers that merely freeing slaves does not make for a utopian or free society. Instead, on the planet she has idealized as a model of individual freedom, a social space has either to be created or taken so that individuals can pursue their own interests.

Rakam is fascinated by the study of history, and, once she escapes from the rice plantation, her mastery of history enables her to rise to prominence in Yeowan society as an expert and a teacher. Her true personal liberation, though, comes only at the end of the story, when she meets Havzhiva, who asks her: "Oh, Rakam! will you let me make love to you?" and she replies: "I want to make love to you…I never did. I never made love to anyone" (Le Guin 1995, 279). In this response, Rakam alludes to her sexual history of being "used" by others without her consent, and occasionally being pursued sexually, but never previously having exercised a sexual choice. As she does so for the first time, Le Guin also implies that freedom is socially constructed, since Rakam's sexual freedom could not have been achieved without Havzhiva as her partner.

In an earlier text, Genly Ai, the narrator of Le Guin's acclaimed *The Left Hand of Darkness* (1969), opens his narrative with the words: "I will make my report as if I told a story." He continues: "for I was taught as a child on my homeworld that Truth is a matter of the imagination" (Le Guin 1969, 9) To a scientist, or anyone with an empiricist approach towards knowledge, the terms "Truth" (with a capital T) and "imagination" appear to be diametrically opposed: after all, "imagination" deals with what is invented and fanciful, whereas "Truth" can be empirically verified. The collocation of these two terms recalls Orhan Pamuk's discussion of the value of reading in his essay "On Reading: Words or Images," where he writes:

> …words (and the works of literature they make) are like water or like ants. Nothing can penetrate into the cracks, holes, and invisible gaps of life as fast or as thoroughly as words can. It is in these cracks

that the essence of things — the things that make us curious about life, about the world — can be ascertained, and it is good literature that first reveals them. (Pamuk 2007, III)

One such gap or crack, we discover on reading *The Left Hand of Darkness*, lies in our understanding of gender difference. As Genly Ai becomes fully acquainted with Gethenian society, where gender difference does not exist for most of the time, he explores the gaps in his own understanding and arrives at a new and more egalitarian view of human nature, which does not divide people of different genders.

While imagination is personal, specific to the individual, "Truth" is supposedly universal. Truth, with a capital T, is true for everyone because everyone experiences it in the same way. Genly Ai's opening statements in *The Left Hand of Darkness*, equating Truth with the imagination, deconstruct the notion of universal truth and replace it with local and individual truths. As if to emphasize the co-existence of different narratives and truths, *The Left Hand of Darkness* contains narratives by several narrators, including the Chiffewarian Investigator Ong Tot Oppong and mythical Gethenian tales of origin and non-origin, as well as the diaries of the two main protagonists, Genly Ai and his Gethenian counterpart, disgraced Karhidian Prime Minister Therem Harth rem ir Estraven. The confluence of all these narratives presents the reader with multiple perspectives on the complex political situation on Gethen, as well as creating a more diverse and rich exploration of its history than if only one narrative were told.

Genly Ai's "report" is an official document, addressed to the Ekumenian authorities who sent him to Gethen as First Mobile to negotiate the planet's joining the Ekumen. Therefore it would appear to belong to the genre of formal writing, dealing with tasks assigned and discharged, rather than to personal narrative. The value of the narrative, though, lies in Genly's personal interactions with Gethenians, his dawning aware-ness of the social and political impact on society of a biology that is not gender-specific, and his concomitant realization and abandonment of his own gender prejudices. Ong Tot Oppong's report on "The Question of Sex" notes that

> A man wants his virility regarded, a woman wants her femininity appreciated, however indirect and subtle the indications of regard and appreciation. On Winter they will not exist. One is respected and judged only as a human being. It is an appalling experience. (Le Guin 1969: 86)

Indeed, Genly Ai is "appalled" to find himself in a society where gender difference, and the accompanying "regard and appreciation," are absent. His frequent use of gender-marked adjectives to describe the Gethenians he meets (such as "Damning [Estraven's] effeminate deviousness" [1969, 19] and "My landlady, a voluble man" [1969, 46]) demonstrate his futile attempts to slot individuals who do not inherently possess gender into a pre-existing framework of gender inequality and domination.

As he journeys across the Gobrin Ice with Estraven, though, he learns appreciation for the Gethenian and, in his own psyche, learns to inte-grate the masculine and feminine aspects of human nature, so that he can write: "I saw then, and for good, what I had always been afraid to see, and had pretended not to see in him: that he was a woman as well as a man.

Any need to explain the sources of that fear vanished with the fear; what I was left with was, at last, acceptance of him as he was. (Le Guin 1969, 210) Genly's personal relationship with Estraven, who alone on Gethen wants to see his world integrated into the Ekumen, leads him to an acknowledgement of gender inequality, and thus to healing the gender divide in his own mind.

At the end of the narrative, a ship is sent to Gethen's surface to fetch Genly, and he sees his fellow travellers for the first time with new eyes: "They all looked strange to me, men and women, well as I knew them. Their voices sounded strange: too deep, too shrill. They were like a troupe of great, strange animals, of two different species: great apes with intelligent eyes, all of them in rut..." (1969, 249). Genly's three years on Gethen have changed his perception of sexuality and gender to the point where it seems unthinkable to have two separate sexes, since he now sees gender as integrated within each individual. This learning and healing comes at a cost, though, and Estraven is killed by mercenaries at the end of their journey, leaving Genly to pay tribute to him in his report.

"The Shobies' Story" offers a more playful deployment of the narrative of healing within the conceptual context of instantaneous space travel. The multicultural crew of the spaceship *The Shoby* are stranded in space when all their instruments mysteriously malfunction. They have oxygen, but no way to pinpoint their location or to return to their home planet. At the beginning of the story, Le Guin stresses the divergent epistemologies of the crew: there is an Anarresti, a Hainish woman, two Gethenians and a few Terrans. Each member of the crew experiences the churten process (an experimental method of travelling instantaneously) in a different way, and they have conflicting sensory impressions of the planet they may (or may not) find at the end of their journey. Shan decides: "We thought we'd tell…what happened…. Each of us. What we — what it seemed like, seems like, to us. So that…" (Le Guin 1994, 108). As the stories unfold, they are heard as mutually exclusive: for example, Tai claims that she did not go to the planet's surface, but her son contradicts her flatly. The child, Asten, brings the collective story into the correct form: "A thousand winters ago, a thousand miles away," or, in consensus terms, as Shan puts it: "Once upon a time…" (Le Guin 1994, 111).

As the story unfolds, following the conventional pattern of narrative, the crew members articulate their unspoken motives and hopes for their joint experiment with the churten drive, and ship's engines begin to hum again. "The Shobies' Story" elegantly demonstrates that individuals can only speak authoritatively about their own experiences and self-stories, and that, as they do, energy is released and movement becomes possible. Without crafting a collective narrative out of their disparate self-stories, the crew would have been lost in space without temporal or spatial coordinates. The act of telling a story, shaping it together, enables them to end the story appropriately: "They got lost. But they found the way" (Le Guin 1994, 113). In the process of narrating their stories, and creating a collective narrative, they devise, and bring about, their "preferred outcome."

Telling stories, weaving narratives, creates meaning and possibilities. As narrative therapists recognize, the act of narration creates the self, but does so in a context where dialectic is inherent in the situation of the self within culture and language:

We gain the self-told narratives that make and remake our selves from the culture in which we live. However much we may rely on a functioning brain to achieve our selfhood, we are virtually from the start expressions of the culture that nurtures us. And culture itself is a dialectic, replete with alternative narratives of what self is or might be. The stories we tell to create ourselves reflect that dialectic. (Bruner 2004, 13)

It is inevitable, given the dialectical relationships between language, identity, and culture, that some narratives, and some selves, will conflict with one another, as they do in "The Shobies' Story." The story demonstrates, though, that it is possible to weave conflicting stories together into a coherent, if not entirely continuous, narrative.

In a similar reconciliation of discontinuities, the farmer Tiokunan'n Hideo, on the planet of O, narrates "Another Story" with the explicit purpose of telling his readers how he experiences two outcomes to his own life. Like Genly Ai, he opens his tale with "I shall make my report as if I told a story, this having been the tradition for some time now" (Le Guin 1994, 159). Hideo is destined by his society's customs for a complex four-way marriage including his childhood sweetheart, Isidri. Nevertheless, he decides to study temporal physics on the distant planet of Hain, knowing that this means he may never return. His choice can be read as a preference for the life of the mind — education — and against the wishes of his family and community, which destine him for a more domestic existence.

Hideo's journey to Hain takes place by instantaneous transmission, using the churten drive tested in "The Shobies' Story," and, as part of his research, he decides to go back home to O for a "skip over and back" (194). But something goes wrong with the transmission, and he finds himself back on O, eighteen years previously. By this time, though, he has narrated his experience of studying physics in isolation and the lack of fulfil-ment it has brought him. This narrative has become part of his self-story and his identity, and he uses it to craft another future, in which he does not go to Hain to study, but stays on O and marries Isidri and another couple in the complex and customary *sedoretu* marriage arrangement.

"Another Story" is most aptly titled, for it narrates how a man, faced with two possible life trajectories, chooses one, then the other. There are two self-stories within its covers, and at the end of them, Hideo is both a farmer on O and an expert in the yet-to-be-developed technology of the churten drive. Hideo renounces the narrative that would have led to renown as a temporal physicist. This narrative would have been coherent and linear. But, as Orhan Pamuk recognizes, human life is neither:

> It doesn't matter if we believe in a grand narrative or indeed in its shadow; both are too clearly delineated to convey the shape of reality. Our lives do not have a center, a single focal point; what goes on inside our heads is too chaotic for us ever to achieve such focus. (2007, 132)

Hideo's early life lacks a "single focal point" because he wants to study temporal physics and also wants to remain on O, marry Isidri and become a farmer. "Another Story" heals the conflict between these two possible self-stories by allowing him to live them both. Like Genly Ai's report, "Another Story" is "a matter of the imagination" as even Hideo recognizes that he cannot have "a life impossibly lived twice" (Le Guin 1994, 203); but it articulates the truth of the consequences of all personal choice, and the desirability of a meaningful position within a community.

While individual narratives (or self-stories) can unfold to the benefit of their subjects, allowing the development of a preferred outcome, language also holds another, more sinister social power in its guise as ideology. Ideology is generally used to subjugate human beings in the service of a predetermined teleology or goal. We only have to think of the "narratives" of Nazism and other forms of totalitarianism to realize how forceful and damaging such discourses can be. In *The Postmodern Condition* (1984), Jean-François Lyotard labels these ideological discourses "grand narratives," adding that they come in two forms: "the life of the spirit and/or the emancipation of humanity" (51).

Le Guin's 2001 novel, *The Telling*, demonstrates the damage to autonomy that follows from slavish adherence to such narratives. On Earth, there has been a religious revolution. A religion named Unism has forged an alliance with governments and declared itself the only acceptable system of thought. The single nature of Unism naturally precludes any other form of religion or thinking, and violent purges of unbelievers and dissenters have followed. A woman evocatively named Sutty (in an echo of the Hindu custom of *sati* or widow-sacrifice) survives the purges, but loses her partner, and is sent as an Observer of the Ekumen to the planet Aka, where Terran missionaries have already spread the narrative of Unism.

On arrival, Sutty is greeted by slogans reading "FORWARD TO THE FUTURE. PRODUCER-CONSUMERS OF AKA MARCH TO THE STARS" and "REACTIONARY THOUGHT IS THE DEFEATED ENEMY" (2001, 7). A single religion has assumed control in the name of "science" and "progress" (closely allied with capitalism, as implied in the term "producer-consumer" applied to all citizens), and government forces are at work to erase all traces of older thought-systems. But Sutty's job is to "go look for these 'stories'; or the people who know them" (26). In Okzat-Ozkat, Sutty finds the believers and practitioners of "the Telling," a system of inter-woven narratives about human and non-human life, culture, heroism, and metaphysics. Her first encounter with the Telling is in the Fertiliser's shop, where the signs appear to be alive: "She had the curious sensation that the pictographs and ideograms that covered the walls with bold black and dark-blue shapes were moving, not jumpily like half-seen print but evenly, regularly, expanding and shrinking very gently, as if they were breathing" (53). The strange impression of organic movement indicates that the signs, and the concepts they denote, are alive, despite the newer conceptual system's attempt to erase them.

Through her friendship with the honoured *"maz,"* or tellers, Sutty discovers an alternative system of thought. She is troubled by its scope and lack of consistency:

> …a way of thinking and living developed and elaborated over thousands of years by the vast majority of human beings on this world, an enormous interlocking system of symbols, metaphors, correspondences, theories, cosmology, cooking, calisthenics, physics, metaphysics, metallurgy, medicine, physiology, psychology, alchemy, chemistry, calligraphy, numerology, herbalism, diet, legend, parable, poetry, history, and story. (91)

In fact, the Telling embraces all aspects of human life within its meta-phorical reach, as Maz Elyed explains patiently:

"I tell, yoz Sutty."

"Yes. But the stories, all the things you tell, what do they do?"

"They tell the world."

"Why, maz?"

"That's what people do, yoz. That's what we're here for." (130)

Sutty is looking for religion, and finds narrative instead. It is not a narrative of transcendence, but immanence, and it is emphatically not a single grand narrative: rather, it is a collection of smaller, divergent and discontinuous local tales. One of the metaphors used to describe it is the forest, which holds many trees and life-forms, all different but all part of a single biome. In this way, it is similar to the hermeneutic philosopher Ricoeur's view of narrative, which

> proposes that narrative is the mental structuring process through which we define our existential relationship to the movements of our earth and the planets, stars and galaxies; to our linear perspective of time typified by the invention of the calendar; to events in the objective and subjective worlds; and to our sense of moving from past to future, through retrospection and anticipation, with the present as a continuing interaction point with both. (Payne 2006, 19)

The smaller pieces of the Telling are similar to what Lyotard calls "the little narrative (*petit récit*) [which] remains the quintessential form of imaginative invention" (1984, 60) and can subvert the dominance of "grand narratives." These little narratives are the only means of resisting the dominance of Unism on Aka, and their preservation is paramount because they encapsulate the sovereignty and creativity of the individuals and communities that practise them. The sacred places of the Telling are libraries, where many narratives are preserved. Sutty's final political act on Aka is to preserve the great library at Silong and to begin decriminalizing the Telling, so that Akans can freely practice the craft of narrative and so shape their world and themselves.

The Telling is a parable about the necessity of narrative for human life to continue. In its internal discontinuities, the multiplicity of its symbols and metaphors, the Telling is a microcosm of our own multiple stories. It encapsulates imagination, creativity, culture, meaning, and individual significance. When Sutty tells her own self-story to the Monitor Yara at Silong, she reaches the healing understanding that her own personal loss of her partner has not been wasted. She also attains a full grasp of her role on Aka as a champion of the Telling. Her healing is achieved when she opposes the dominating "grand narrative" of Unism and aligns herself with the "little narratives," including her own, that make up human life.

Since the publication of *The Telling*, Ursula K. Le Guin has crafted several narratives of self-making and social healing (such as *Gifts*, *Voices*, *Powers*, and *Lavinia*). Each of her tales offers the reader an excursion into the creative and healing power of narrative, without which human beings would be bereft of a method of making sense of our selves or the world in which we live.

BIBLIOGRAPHY

Bruner, Jerome. 2004. "The Narrative Creation of Self." In Lynne E. Angus and John McLeod (eds). *The Handbook of Narrative and Psychotherapy: Practice, Theory, and Research*. London and New Delhi: Sage Publications, 3–14.

Freedman, Jill and Gene Combs. 1996. *Narrative Therapy: The Social Construction of Preferred Realities*. New York and London: W. W. Norton & Company.

Le Guin, Ursula K. 1969 (rpt. 1992). *The Left Hand of Darkness*. London: Orbit.

————. 1989. *Dancing at the Edge of the World: Thoughts on Words, Women, Places*. London: Victor Gollancz.

————. 1994. *A Fisherman of the Inland Sea: Science Fiction Stories*. New York: HarperPaperbacks.

————. 1995. *Four Ways to Forgiveness: Stories*. New York: HarperCollins.

————. 2001. *The Telling*. New York: Ace Books.

Lyotard, Jean-François. Trans. Geoff Bennington and Brian Massumi. 1984. *The Postmodern Condition: A Report on Knowledge*. Theory and History of Literature, Vol. 10. Manchester: Manchester University Press.

Pamuk, Orhan. Trans. Maureen Freely. 2007. *Other Colours: Essays and a Story*. London: Faber and Faber.

Payne, Martin. 2006. *Narrative Therapy: An Introduction for Counsellors*. 2nd edition. London and New Delhi: Sage Publications.

Ricoeur, Paul. 1984. *Time and Narrative*. Chicago: University of Chicago Press.

Why I Love "Direction of the Road"

SUZETTE HADEN ELGIN

IT'S HARD FOR ME to describe the impact this story had on me when it first appeared in 1974, when I was a newbie linguistics prof at San Diego State University. No short story I have ever read, in all my life, has affected me as forcibly as this one did. All the time I was reading it, I kept thinking, "This can't be happening! I can't be reading a short story that's narrated by a tree!"

Which will immediately make it clear to you that I'm not one of those people who started reading sf as a child and never stopped; people like that wouldn't have been surprised that an sf short story was being narrated by a tree. I didn't start reading sf until I was in my early thirties and had to find a genre I could earn money writing, so that I could pay my tuition and my bills.

I love "Direction of the Road" because it is the most fantastic of all fantasies. Trees, it tells us, are able to go in two directions at the same time — always growing larger for those coming toward them, always shrinking for those going away from them, at the same time — even when there are dozens of different entities to deal with, all at the same time. Can you imagine that? Can you get your head around that? I can't. My brain and my mind aren't nearly powerful enough.

I love "Direction of the Road" for its word-coinings: "the loose creatures" [humans and other animals]; "a making" [a constructed object, like cars and wagons and the road itself]; "an unliving creature" [all the makings].

I love "Direction of the Road" because you really — truly — perceive the universe through the worldview of the tree that is the narrator. It's hard enough to write a short story that makes it possible for readers to perceive the universe as it's perceived by someone of their own gender and their own ethnic group and their own various persuasions. "Direction of the Road" goes way beyond that; it lets you *be* a tree. For me, it gives a whole new semantic dimension to the troublesome concept of "cultural appropriation."

I love "Direction of the Road" because I still don't fully understand the ending even after all these years, but each glimpse of understanding I add when I read the story again is valuable and teaches me more; I hope to fully understand it before I die.

My favorite snip from the story is on page 269 (of the Harper Perennial edition of *The Compass Rose*):

> The apple trees in the orchard at the foot of the hill did not seem to mind; but then, apples are tame. Their genes have been tampered with for centuries. Besides, they are herd creatures; no orchard tree can really form an opinion of its own.

I love and I savor that last bit: "no orchard tree can really form an opinion of its own."

I am so grateful for "Direction of the Road."

"From Elfland to Poughkeepsie" and Back Again

or, I think we're in Poughkeepsie now, Toto

LISA TUTTLE

EIGHT OR NINE YEARS AGO I was commissioned to write a book with the self-explanatory title *Writing Fantasy & Science Fiction*. In the first draft of one chapter, I quoted so extensively from Ursula K. Le Guin that the editor felt obliged to intervene, mentioning that people buying my book would expect to get *my* advice on the subject, and not to be told, at length, what another writer had said, no matter how fervently I agreed with it. I took her point. *Steering the Craft*, Ursula's very lucid and helpful writing-workshop-between-two-covers, had been published a couple of years earlier, and nobody needed me as an inefficient go-between, cutting up her well-reasoned arguments and sprinkling little bits of them throughout my own.

So I thought a little harder about what I wanted to say, wrote more directly out of my own experience as a reader, writer and editor, and removed most of the quotations — although I still used the beginning of *The Dispossessed* (because it was perfect) as a good example of the narrative strategy often called "omniscient" (Ursula suggests "involved author").

Realizing that much of my own thinking about fantasy fiction had been shaped by one particular piece written by Ursula, I made that clear in the section on "Style," writing:

"The best essay I can think of on the subject of style and fantasy is 'From Elfland to Poughkeepsie' by Ursula K. Le Guin. I urge you to find a copy and read it. Although the market for commercial fantasy has expanded hugely since she wrote her essay in 1973, everything she said then is still relevant today."

Looking back, remembering the early '70s, it seems to me now that fantasy, as a genre, scarcely existed in those days. A story with magic in it, or dragons, or set in a made-up world, was, like a fairy tale, suitable only for children (unless, like the librarian quoted in "Why Are Americans Afraid of Dragons?": "we don't feel escapism is good for children"). So firm was the connection fantasy = childish that when in 1969 Betty Ballantine and Lin Carter began a new imprint it was "Ballantine Adult Fantasy." Maybe the x-rated connotation wasn't so strongly connected with the word "adult" as it is now?

But even more than thirty years ago, as Ursula so presciently noted,

A great many people want to go there [Elfland], without knowing what it is they're really looking for, driven by a vague hunger for something real. With the intention or under the pretense of obliging them, certain writers of fantasy are building six-lane highways and trailer parks with drive-in movies, so that the tourists can feel at home just as if they were back in Poughkeepsie.

But the point about Elfland is that you are not at home there. It's not Poughkeepsie. It's different.

By now (writing in this still science fictional-sounding year of 2009), Elfland seems to have been entirely paved over and strip-malled to death, stuffed with fast-food restaurants and tourist hotels, the local inhabitants prohibited from using their own language, forced to labor in sex-shops or factories…oops, sorry, I'm in danger of being carried away by my bête noir. Today's Americans are far from being afraid of dragons; rather they expect to buy them cheap and often, like the guns and cars it's supposedly our god-given right to own. And in an atmosphere of computer-generated imagery and popular culture, much that was special and strange about Elfland has become, like personal eroticism, standardized, commercialized, mass-produced, and soulless as porn.

Amid all this, true fantasy, the real thing, the good stuff, is still being written. There may be more good fantasy available now than ever before, simply because there's a market for it. A book (good or bad) may be turned down for many reasons, but that it contains dragons or elf-lords and is not set in the "real world" now makes it more rather than less commercially desirable. But, as Ursula told us, decades before evil spells and dark lords and schools for wizards had become the common currency they are now — "a writer may use all the trappings of fantasy without ever actually imagining anything."

And why would a writer do such a thing? Why are there so many badly-written, ineptly imagined books bearing the imprint of "Fantasy"? Well, to quote Ursula again (no editor can stop me now. I am here to praise Ursula, and to quote her):

> Well, undoubtedly avarice is one of the reasons. Fantasy is selling well, so let's all grind out a fantasy. The Old Baloney Factory. And sheer ineptness enters in. But in many cases neither greed nor lack of skill seems to be involved, and in such cases I suspect a failure to

take the job seriously: a refusal to admit what you're in for when you set off with only an ax and a box of matches into Elfland.

A fantasy is a journey. It is a journey into the subconscious mind, just as psychoanalysis is. Like psychoanalysis, it can be dangerous; and it will change you.

Most genre fantasy is, of course, nothing of the kind. It's not dangerous, unless as the psychic equivalent of eating deep-fried Mars bars. I think something important was lost when fantasy became "Fantasy," a generic label that makes it particularly hard to talk about something basic in the human psyche because now the cheap'n'easy stuff so far outnumbers the serious journeying that anyone who wants to talk about "fantasy" with the seriousness that Ursula accorded it is constantly having to redefine the term.

I've been thinking about "life-changing" books. Everyone who reads, whether or not they'd use the term "life-changing" [my husband, for example, would not], could name some precious titles, books they'll never forget. Children's books, and classics assigned at school, generally feature large on these lists when the public is asked to respond, and I don't think that's because a lot of people never read another book after leaving school — those people aren't likely to bother to answer. I've certainly read many good, even great, books over the past thirty years, but if I'm asked for the books that have been most important to me, I always go back to what I read when I was young. I doubt I'd include anything I read after the age of twenty-four, simply because those early books shaped me in a way that just wasn't possible later on. I became who I am at least in part because of the books I read, and insofar as "who I am" is a writer, that's even more emphatically true.

When I said I'd write something for this festschrift, I intended it to be about Ursula's writings on writing. I thought of *Steering the Craft* (1998), such a useful toolkit that every aspiring and practicing writer should own a copy — her discussion of point of view is especially good, and after reading her "Opinion Piece on Narrative Tense" I finally understood why I generally dislike novels written in the present tense (a.k.a. "focussed narrative tense"). I also thought of some of the essays in *Dancing at the Edge of the World: Thoughts on Words, Women, Places* (1989), particularly "Some Thoughts on Narrative" (1980), "The Carrier Bag Theory of Fiction" (1986), and "The Fisherwoman's Daughter" (1988), although, right from the start, I knew I mainly wanted to re-read and then write about *The Language of the Night: Essays on Fantasy and Science Fiction* (1979), a book that I've loved and savored and turned to many times over the years, carrying it with me from Austin to Houston to London to Devon, back to London, and then bringing it here to Scotland, nineteen years ago.

But when I began, I found that I mostly wanted to talk about just one essay from that book: "From Elfland to Poughkeepsie." It was this essay that I'd so compulsively quoted from when I first tried my hand at writing about writing fantasy. It's this essay that's lodged so deeply in my thoughts about writing (and reading) fantasy that I can't distinguish my ideas from hers. What did I think about the importance of fantasy before I encountered Ursula's ideas? I have no idea. I couldn't even remember when, or where, I first read it, although I had a strong feeling that it was already familiar to me in 1979 when I bought my hardback copy of *The Language of the Night* new from Garner & Smith in Austin.

From the copyright page I learned that "From Elfland to Poughkeepsie" was first published in 1973 as a chapbook by the Pendragon Press. I know I never owned a copy. (If I did, I'd still have it.) Then, in Susan Wood's introduction: "This essay…originated as a talk given to the Second Science Fiction Writers' Workshop (the Clarion West workshop) at the University of Washington in 1972."

How could I have forgotten? I was there. I was one of the student-writers at that Clarion, nineteen years old in the summer of 1972, and eagerly, hungrily absorbing everything I could about the art and craft of writing. The professionals guiding us were Avram Davidson, Ursula K. Le Guin, Robert Silverberg, Harlan Ellison, Terry Carr, and Frank Herbert. My first experience of "From Elfland to Poughkeepsie" was not of words on paper, but the words spoken by their author. Magic words. They fell on my ear, and I made them my own.

Life-changing, yes, absolutely.

2 SEPTEMBER 2009, TORINTURK, SCOTLAND

The Closet

JOHN KESSEL

CARSON came out of the closet naked, holding his riding shorts in his right hand and carrying his bike shoes in his left. He dropped the shoes by the side of the bed, pulled on the shorts, got a bike shirt and socks from the dresser.

Over a breakfast of orange juice and toast he read the morning paper, checking out the sports and op ed pages. No chance for health care reform, and good riddance. Yankees beat the Sox to move into first.

He went out to the garage, raised the door and wheeled his bike out around the Porsche. His bicycle was a 2007 Jamis Ventura Elite, super-light full carbon composite with Vittoria Zaffiro tires. He pulled on his gloves, settled his shades on the bridge of his nose, strapped on his helmet, mounted, and rode off down the street toward the greenway.

It was early enough that the greenway wasn't too crowded, and he built up some speed listening to the whir of the chain and the hum of the tires on the pavement. The wind whistled past his ears, carrying the sound of birdsong. He got a good rhythm going. As he approached the lake, however, the number of joggers and dog walkers and seniors and young mothers with strollers increased. Most of them oblivious, wandering all over the path, wrapped up in their precious brats, blissfully uncaring that they were sharing the public pavement with anyone.

He used his bell to alert them as he came up from behind. "Passing on your left!" he called out each time. Some of them started comically. Others jerked their dogs' leashes. Some turned their heads to look before moving to the right. The worst were the joggers with iPods plugged into their ears who would not have heard him unless he threw a stick of dynamite as he came up from behind. He sometimes wished for a stick of dynamite.

Near the end of the ride, he was moving along swiftly, his mind on work (he could see already he was going to be late), coming up on a woman with a stroller in the middle of the path. He shifted to the left to go by, but just as he approached he saw the woman had the toddler out of the stroller. She let the kid go and it staggered directly into his path.

"I'm passing!" he shouted. The woman jerked the kid's arm and fell over. Carson sped by. The baby started screaming. In his mirror he watched the woman clutch the bawling kid to her breast. He powered on up the last hill, and past that to the street and his condo.

Because of the bike ride he was an hour late getting to the office. But it was Friday, and his boss was a wuss, always begging Carson to go full-time, and Carson didn't give a fuck. He wrote the best copy in the department, always finished his product on time. The clients, whom he alternately charmed or bullied, either loved or were afraid of him. So what if he was only there three days a week? They never complained.

He was writing a TV ad for an erectile dysfunction drug. His angle was different — instead of images of fit, blue-jeans-wearing men in their fifties with good hair, he went for a schlub guy thirty pounds overweight wearing a Giants jersey in a sports bar. On the big screen TV the Giants, losing big to the Eagles, line up for a field goal and miss, wide right. While the rest of the fans in the bar piss and moan, his wife, equally overweight, wearing a matching jersey, tosses off a shot and leans across the table to whisper in Mr. Schlub's ear. They both get up and head for the Ladies. Voiceover: "You never know when that special moment will come."

Halfway through the day he got a call from Clarice, his ex. Where was the last alimony check, she wanted to know. The school year started in another week and Ashton needed new clothes.

"You'll get your check," he said.

"I need the money now, not next month."

"I know what you need, and it's not money. And it's not something anybody else can give you."

"Carson, if you don't —"

"I can't talk to you." He hung up.

His stomach churned throughout the afternoon. Clarice, pouring poison into Ashton's ear, always made him feel that way, a complex stew of anxiety, resentment, and rage.

When he went into the break room for coffee, one of the new account girls was there whacking a jar of pickles against the counter. "Can you open this for me?" she asked. Carson had very strong hands; he took the jar and broke the seal on the lid easily.

"Thanks," she said.

"Don't mention it." She had a big nose with a bend in it, but she was still cute.

He felt better the rest of the afternoon. The last half hour of the workday he spent checking his email and watching the clock. As soon as it was five he hit the elevators down to the lot and headed for happy hour at The Hound and Hare.

He had two manhattans and scanned the bar room. The din of people

218 · MEMORIES & REFLECTIONS

shouting over the loud music pounded into his head. He had a little buzz on and the beginnings of a headache. There was a brunette with large brown eyes and too much eye makeup seated at a table with a dishwater blonde. The blonde got up and went to talk to some guy in a pink polo shirt. Carson carried his drink over to the table.

"I'm Carson," he said.

The brunette had watched him approach, and apparently he passed muster. "Linda."

"I'd like to kiss you, Linda. Would that be okay?"

"Fuck off, Carson."

They ended up in the front seat of his Porsche in the corner of the parking deck, beside a concrete pillar with a big purple "3" stenciled on it. The light was dim. They struggled with her pantyhose. Her breath smelled of cigarettes, but her breasts were large with dark brown areolas. Afterward she rolled off him into the passenger seat. "That was good," she said.

"Yeah, it was," Carson said.

"Do you come to the bar often?"

"Pretty often."

She had her purse open and was brushing her hair. "Maybe I'll see you again."

"If you recognize me," he said. She looked at him funny, and decided to laugh. He walked her to her car, and after she drove away stood at the edge of the deck, looking out over the lights of the city. The sound of traffic, smell of exhaust. Red tail lights on the interstate that swerved through the heart of town. He realized he was angry, that he was always angry. He had been cheated, and he did not understand how or why.

Beside his black wingtip was a white pebble. He picked it and dropped it over the side of the deck, watching as it fell three stories and bounced on the sidewalk. Look out below!

He checked his Rolex. It was 10:23.

He went back to his car and drove home, his stomach grinding against his backbone. From the refrigerator he took a slice of honey-baked ham and ate it with a hard roll, standing up at the kitchen counter.

After brushing his teeth, he stripped off his clothes and threw them into the basket just inside the closet door. He stood naked in front of the full-length mirror on the door and examined himself. He looked okay. He looked pretty decent for a man of his age.

Still, he was sick of it. He reached up under his chin, split the skin over his Adam's apple, drew open the seam straight down his chest and belly, parting the flesh. Shrugged shoulders out from under muscles, grabbed the thick black hair and pulled the face, grinning grotesquely as it stretched and distorted, up over the smooth head beneath it, and stepped out of the body. The balls had turned inside out; it took a good shake of the male envelope until its genitals flopped and hung straight. Stepping into the closet, Carson hung this body next to the other, the one with the breasts and flawless skin and long, pale blonde hair.

Turn out the light and get into bed.

Old Friend

JUDITH BARRINGTON

SHARED MEMORIES jump and flash like old movies:
the spray of sand arcing behind a car
on the track that leads to the pillars of Rome;
ponies grazing beyond a motel window
as someone deals cards and somebody laughs;
osprey diving from a lookout tree
across the river with its animal rocks —
humpbacks swimming alongside the writer's deck.

An old friend can never be taken for granite:
to know and be known is a softer, more crumbly rock.
Sometimes it nests in the creek bed, oval
like a fragile egg that will crack and shatter
when something hurtles downstream in the spate:
wind-cracked spruce, old bridge, a whirl of words.

Solitude and Souls

NISI SHAWL

WHEN I WAS A CHILD, my family was too poor to provide me with a room of my own. I wanted one with the quiet desperation only children entertain — the desperation of those powerless yet full of desires.

I never got my own room until I became an adult. I was twenty-one. I painted the walls lavender and the trim in a pale turquoise satin-gloss. Though an adult, I remembered then and remember even now everything of importance in my childhood: all my feelings, all my fears and wishes. And this is probably why Ursula K. Le Guin's story "Solitude" speaks so meaningfully to me.

"Solitude" is part of the Hainish cycle. It is presented as an addendum to the report of an Observer, a field ethnologist who brought her children on her assignment to the planet Eleven-Soros. The addendum is by the field ethnologist's daughter.

Human society on Eleven-Soros is, by some standards, broken. Emotional engagement is viewed negatively and avoided, and adult-to-adult contact kept to a strict minimum. The field ethnologist's report, titled "Poverty," apparently reflects her view on what's lacking; the daughter, Serenity, has a different take. Serenity appreciates silence, fears and loathes the entanglements of loyalty, jealousy, so forth, so on. Instead of playing house or store or school or any of the socializing games I played with other children, she "slow-walks" and "starwatches": "that is when you lie down on the open hills in the dry season at night, and find a certain star in the eastern sky, and watch it across the sky till it sets. You can look away, of course, to rest your eyes, and to doze, but you try to keep looking back at the star and the stars around it, until you feel the earth turning, until you become aware of how the stars and the world and the soul move together."

"The soul" is what Serenity is making. In Serenity's cosmos people don't have souls. Only persons do. And only if they make them.

I asked Ursula whether Eleven-Soros was a dystopia or a utopia. "For this one," she answered, "it would be heaven."

I asked her that question when we were together, face-to-face, but I can't really remember exactly when that was: when Eileen Gunn and I interviewed her for a television show Vonda N. McIntyre produced ("Science Fiction Conversations," for the record — available online at *www.sfconversations.com/*)? After her speech at the Seattle Public Library upon her acceptance of the Maxine Cushing Gray Fellowship for Writers? Or was it when I had lunch with her and maybe twenty other people at an Indian restaurant in Seattle's Wallingford neighborhood — a highly social occasion? It was certainly before my first visit to her home in Portland, last January. I went there with Kath Wilham, an editor at Aqueduct Press, to help in picking out illustrations for the other Ursula K. Le Guin work I want to talk about here.

Cheek by Jowl collects some of Ursula's essays on children's literature — and the fantastic — and animals. In the title essay she talks about how certain stories reflect and strengthen the connection between us and the wild, a connection missing from most people's everyday lives. She quotes Hugh Lofting's Dr. Doolittle as saying: "So long as the birds and the beasts and the fishes are my friends, I do not have to be afraid...." This book is about community, the ties that bind us one to another, across the boundaries of species, even.

In that essay's conclusion she writes, "We go crazy in solitude." A contradiction? Wasn't the world of "Solitude" her idea of heaven? But in the paragraph above that sentence she describes a situation only a little short of the crisis that precipitated the invalidation of Eleven-Soros's social contract: "We come ever closer to isolating ourselves, a solitary species swarming on a desert world."

Isolation is different from solitude. It is enforced, not chosen. It is a form of torture, one our government inflicts with impunity on prisoners. In prolonged isolation, our brain waves slow, and our brains develop abnormalities as severe as those exhibited by sufferers of head injuries.

It's isolation Ursula is talking about in *Cheek by Jowl*. Solitary confinement, which is not at all the same as solitude.

Earlier in the essay Ursula speaks of the invention of Nature-with-a-capital-N in eighteenth century Europe, a concept comprising "all the other species and all the places where they live and we don't.... Nature is humanity's Other." As an Other, Nature is demonized, idealized, exoticized, subordinated, objectified, distanced, lessened in a hundred thousand ways. To the extent any of us participate in this Othering, we lock ourselves out of community with the species with whom we share this world. And we lock ourselves *into* a tiny, tiny cell that defines what we mean by "us." Solitary.

Brought back against her will to the ship orbiting Eleven-Soros, Serenity finds no place to be alone and make her soul:

Of course we each had a room; though small, the *Heyho* was a Hainish-built explorer, designed to give its people room and privacy and comfort and variety and beauty.... But it was designed. It was all human-made — everything was human.... I felt the pressure of people all around me, all the time. People around me, people with me, people pressing on me, pressing me to be one of them, to be one of them, one of the people.

Serenity feels as if she is in a trap. There is no room in her environment for anything — *anyone* — besides what is human. To make her soul she needs to go beyond that limitation.

What lies beyond the limitations that humanity defines itself with? Community. Again in "Cheek by Jowl," Ursula writes of kinship with our elders, the species who came before us. Prior to the Othering of nature, of the wild, "We knew we were different, but we knew also that we belonged." The yearning we feel, most especially as children, to "walk with the animals and talk with the animals," like Lofting's Doolittle or Kipling's Mowgli or E. B. White's Fern, must be satisfied, Ursula tells us, "if we want to stay sane and stay alive."

My turquoise-and-lavender room was in a house full of humans, with two cats and a mess of plants. But mainly it was a home for humans. Past the wall I had painted lay a social space. In the years that followed I had my own room again a few more times, but not until 1997 did I have my entire own apartment. I settled into my solitude there like a bath of chocolate mousse. I enjoyed that bath for twelve years, then moved into a smaller, shared space again in March of this year, 2009, mainly for economic reasons.

Now my experiences of solitude are rare again, and more prized than ever. I'm in the midst of one as I write this, at Fort Worden State Park, near Port Townsend, Washington. Yesterday afternoon I drove over from Seattle with poet JT Stewart. We each have a week here as part of Centrum's creative residency program. As I type this I'm looking out my window at the darkening sky over the darkening sea, where tiny, far-off ships glide by, gleaming with light and humanity. It's good to know they're there. They're there and I'm here.

Also nearby are deer, river otters, bald eagles, towhees, song sparrows, and plenty of other neighbors I have yet to meet.

If I stand up and walk to any of the empty rooms on the other side of this apartment, I can look out of their windows and see the house JT is occupying during her residency. By the lamps she switches on I can tell whether she's in the kitchen eating or the bedroom writing. I haven't actually seen JT herself all day. I assume that whatever else she's doing, she's making her soul.

The two of us spent a few hours together yesterday while I drove, exchanging anecdotes and memories. I tried to describe Michigan's Sleeping Bear Dunes to her. It's a favorite place of mine, and a favorite exercise in description to attempt.

The dunes are hundreds of feet high. "Hundreds of feet high," I told her, "straight down to the water. You can run right down the dunes, and each stride you take becomes enormous, ten feet long, and you can't hurt yourself because the sand's so soft." Plunging down the curved brown sides of Sleeping Bear in wind and sun and veils of silica lifted shining in the air, the motion slow and inevitable and fast and down in laughter, breath, heat, and light to the blue, the blue, the blue —

"I suppose you get a tremendous sense of power out of doing that?" JT asked me.

I thought about it.

"No," I said, "not exactly." I thought a little harder. "It's more like the power is in the land. Like you're surrounded by power and it's protecting you because you're part of it. And you can't be hurt, because the sand is soft, it's so soft, and it's holding you and taking care of you. It has the power and you are in it."

BIBLIOGRAPHY

Gawande, Atul: "Hellhole," pp. 36–45, *The New Yorker*, New York, NY, March 30, 2009.

Le Guin, Ursula K.: "Cheek by Jowl," pp. 43–107, *Cheek by Jowl*, 2009, Aqueduct Press, Seattle, WA.

Le Guin, Ursula K.: "Solitude." First published in *The Magazine of Fantasy & Science Fiction*, December, 1994. Reprinted in *The Very Best of Fantasy & Science Fiction*, Gordon Van Gelder (editor), 2009, Tachyon Publications, San Francisco, CA.

For Ursula

ÉLISABETH VONARBURG

I FIRST MET URSULA in a book called *La Main gauche de la nuit*, in 1970, a French translation. So, she was speaking French. I first met her closer, in English, in a book called *The Left Hand of Darkness* — the original — in 1974, I think. Somehow she made even more sense in English. And I first met Ursula in person at the Toronto Harbourfront Literary Festival, in 1986, where she was to present her new novel *Always Coming Home*.

Which one is the true encounter? They all are, of course.

But some first times are firster than others. Harbourfront was *it*. Judith Merril had just edited the first Canadian SF&F anthology, *Tesseracts*. A story of mine was in it. I was to read from it. For me, it had been a terrible year so far, and this was the only ray of sunshine in the pervasive doom and gloom. Not the perspective of reading in English a bit of my story — no, I was petrified — but the perspective of meeting *Ursula Le Guin*. She did exist! Some writers change your life — there is no uncliché-ed way of saying this. *The Left Hand of Darkness* had given me permission to write what I wanted, what I needed to write — even though I wouldn't fully realize it for years, years of continuing conversation with it in my heart and mind. I am still conversing with that book. All of us of my generation who met Ursula there still are, I believe. So many of us at the same time. Did you know, Ursula, how ubiquitous you are?

But there you were, on the podium, an actual, breathing Ursula. Reading for us, in the cavernous hall the festival had been forced to rent, the usual theater being way too small for the huge audience (we SF&FITES were all smirking about that). I was in the first or second row, spellbound. Memory is a weird thing. To this day, I don't recall that you did read from *Always Coming Home*. I remember you reading a short story called "She Unnamed Them," about a grumpy man and his silent wife. And she's Eve, he's Adam, and she unnames the beasts, the plants, the whole world, setting them free again, at last. Even that I am not sure of, now! Perhaps it was something else, and I am conflating several readings of yours. All I recall is that I wept, that time. Wept for joy, wept for beauty. Not for sadness. Never for sadness. You're one of the very few writers who can make me weep. Each time.

About ten years ago, I was asked to tell my favorite story for the French radio, a local show, half an hour long, and I chose *The Left Hand of Darkness*, of course, albeit in French. It was heaven revisiting the novel pen in hand, taking notes, finding everything as I remembered it — and also at once new and fresh, suffused with even more meaning. And it was hell trying to fit all that I loved in it in the limits I had been given to tell the story, because it is so much more than "a story" for me (what about the writing? what about the mood?). I wasn't allowed to read excerpts, but I persuaded the producer to let me read the very ending, when "the boy, Therem's son, said stammering: 'Will you tell us how he died? Will you tell us about the other worlds out among the stars — the other kind of men, the other lives?'" And, even reading it in French, my voice broke completely when we taped that part, and we had to do it all over again. Just typing this, I am tearing up. Pfah, an old, respectable lady of my age!

But I am forever as old as I was when I first read it. And you forever as ageless as you were when I met you there.

After that momentous reading, we ended up…somewhere, with Judy and Candas Dorsey — who was to become a dear friend ever after, and who has a way better, detailed memory of all of this than I do. There certainly were other people too. I don't remember them clearly. I only remember a room, a huge sofa, and you, plopped down into the sofa. We must have talked, all of us. Candas says we even danced. I don't recall. I think I was still high. Then you left, going back to your hotel, and a few moments later Judith asked us what we found the most striking about you. For a very brief instant I hesitated between your laughter and your size, but the latter won. No doubt because my mother was also a small woman, I had just seen her, back there in France, and I was primed for that — thought I. So: "She's so small!" I sighed. I didn't mean that you were supposed to be ten feet tall — I was slightly beyond that then, having already met Judith four years earlier and danced with her. I meant…I meant…I didn't quite know what I meant. And I cringed, because Judith frowned at me — like she expected better — and said sternly: "She's so strong."

Only later, thinking back, did I realize that it was exactly what I meant. And for the laughter, too.

I have two hilarious photos taken at WisCon, in 2006, where you were the GoH: you with the very tall Geoff Ryman towering over you, and then the next one: he's kneeling before you. You are laughing. In the picture, we are all laughing. But in our hearts, we were all there at your feet with him. I know I still am, will always be. It is not subservience. Not even allegiance. Is it knowing that you are the measure of what I am and do as a writer and a person — and so I can never be as tall as you are.

The Soft Key

SANDRA KASTURI

for Ursula K. Le Guin,
who taught me to love the written word

(1)

STILL THE socks and spoons, the hollow rattle
of domestication; hush husbands to bed,
churn daughters toward their rooms, the battle
unending as the pages tick-turn in your head.
Still their voices, their terrible beloved voices,
entangling the shoelaces and the heart-valves;
daily life become molasses-dream slow, no choice
but to grit and grimace while longing for a salve
to soothe the gnawing landlocked beast inside
that strains and leaps toward solitary joy —
the balm of books, each a gloried ride
through a strange world — a key, a beacon, a buoy.
Let drop tea towels and houses and spouses;
let rain the imagination's unruly carouses.

(ii)

See? Here is freedom, strange as irregular
knitting. The other side of the wall is static
with bald poets, wry madmen and bizarre
women flapping their arms in the attic.
Compasses whirl past north and back again.
Roads take or don't take, forests fly through space
and the islands are beset by dragons.
Dragons! Each gold-flickered eye, each trace
of translucent wing, a saw or song to the heart.
Is this the key, then? The door unclicked and swung
open, the oracle with her lips apart?
Or is it shut? Oiled and locked and the last bell rung?
Open the door, close the door, no matter —
the key turns both ways, toward before and after.

(iii)

A flock of thoughts curves down the horizon:
you back at your kitchen window, congealed
as a waxen effigy amongst the pans,
your head full of the latest invented world.
Foxgloves dip and foxpaws pad in the gloaming;
the hums and haws of crickets haven't quite
begun, nor the varied voices combing
through the house. For now, a slow respite,
time enough for keys to soften doorways,
to lie between the clean white leaves of books,

spoon and nibble dappled words and graze
on chapters caught without net or hook.
Let pages turn as they may and locks come undone;
Let one world unravel, as another's begun.

Ursula K. Le Guin: short bibliography

(*Major works only; principal u.s. editions only*)

NOVELS

NOVELS OF THE EKUMEN:

The Telling. Harcourt 2000, Gollancz 2001.

The Word for World is Forest. Putnam 1976, Berkley 1976.

The Dispossessed: An Ambiguous Utopia. Harper & Row 1974,
     Avon 1975.

The Left Hand of Darkness. Walker 1969, Ace 1969, Harper & Row 1980.

City of Illusions. Ace 1967, Harper & Row 1978.

Planet of Exile. Ace 1966, Harper & Row 1978.

Rocannon's World. Ace 1966, Harper & Row 1977.

(These three reissued in one volume as *Worlds of Exile and Illusion*,
     Tor 1998).

THE BOOKS OF EARTHSEA:

The Other Wind. Harcourt 2001.

Tales from Earthsea. Harcourt 2001.

Tehanu. Atheneum 1990, Bantam 1991.

The Farthest Shore. Atheneum 1972, Bantam 1975.

The Tombs of Atuan. Atheneum 1970, Bantam 1975.

A Wizard of Earthsea. Parnassus/Houghton Mifflin 1968, Ace 1970,
     Atheneum 1991.

THE ANNALS OF THE WESTERN SHORE:
Powers. Harcourt, 2007.
Voices. Harcourt, 2006.
Gifts. Harcourt, 2004.

OTHER NOVELS:
Lavinia, Harcourt 2008.
Always Coming Home. Harper & Row 1985, Bantam 1987,
    University of California Press 2000.
The Eye of the Heron. Harper & Row 1983, Bantam 1983.
The Beginning Place. Harper & Row 1980, Bantam 1981.
Malafrena. Putnam 1979, Berkley 1980.
Very Far Away from Anywhere Else. Atheneum 1976, Bantam 1978.
The Lathe of Heaven. Scribners 1971, Avon 1972, Scribners 2008.

STORY COLLECTIONS
Changing Planes, Harcourt 2003.
The Birthday of the World. HarperCollins 2002.
Unlocking the Air. HarperCollins 1996.
Four Ways to Forgiveness. Harper Prism 1995, pb 1996.
A Fisherman of the Inland Sea. Harper Prism 1994. pb 1995.
Searoad. HarperCollins 1991, pb.1992.
Buffalo Gals. Capra 1987, NAL 1988.
The Compass Rose. Underwood-Miller 1982, Harper & Row 1982,
    Bantam 1983.
Orsinian Tales. Harper & Row 1976, Bantam 1977.
The Wind's Twelve Quarters. Harper & Row 1975, Bantam 1976.

POETRY

Incredible Good Fortune. Shambhala 2006.

Sixty Odd. Shambhala 1999.

Going out with Peacocks. HarperCollins 1994.

Blue Moon over Thurman Street. with Roger Dorband, NewSage 1993.

Wild Oats and Fireweed. Harper & Row 1988.

Hard Words. Harper & Row 1981.

Wild Angels. Capra 1974.

TRANSLATIONS

Lao Tzu: Tao Te Ching. Shambhala 1997

The Twins, The Dream/Las Gemelas, El Sueño, with Diana Bellessi.
    Arte Publico Press 1997, Editorial. Norma 1998.

Kalpa Imperial, by Angelica Gorodischer. Small Beer Press 2003.

Selected Poems of Gabriela Mistral. University of New Mexico Press
    2003.

CRITICISM

Cheek by Jowl. Aqueduct 2009.

The Wave in the Mind. Shambhala 2004.

Steering the Craft. Eighth Mountain 1998.

The Language of the Night (revised ed.). HarperCollins 1992.

Dancing at the Edge of the World. Grove 1989.

BOOKS FOR CHILDREN

THE CATWINGS BOOKS:

Jane on her Own. Orchard 1999.

Wonderful Alexander and the Catwings. Orchard 1994.

Catwings Return. Orchard 1989.

Catwings. Orchard 1988.

OTHER BOOKS FOR CHILDREN:

Cat Dreams. Scholastic 2009.

Tom Mouse (illus J. Downing). Roaring Brook 2002.

A Ride on the Red Mare's Back (illus. J. Downing). Orchard 1992, pb 1993.

Fish Soup (illus. P. Wynne). Atheneum 1992.

Fire and Stone (illus. L. Marshall). Atheneum 1989.

A Visit from Dr. Katz (illus. A. Barrow). Atheneum 1988.

Solomon Leviathan (illus. A. Austin). Philomel 1988.

Cobbler's Rune (illus. A. Austin). Cheap Street 1983.

Leese Webster (illus. James Brunsman). Atheneum 1979.

SCREENPLAY IN BOOK FORMAT

King Dog. Capra 1985.

CHAPBOOKS

The Art of Bunditsu. Ygor & Buntho Make Books Press 1993.

Findings. Ox Head 1992.

No Boats. Ygor & Buntho Make Books Press 1992.

A Winter Solstice Ritual for the Pacific Northwest, with Vonda N.
    McIntyre. Ygor & Buntho 1991.

In the Red Zone, with Henk Pander. Lord John 1983.

Tillai and Tylissos, with Theodora Kroeber. Red Bull 1979.

Walking in Cornwall. n.p. 1976. Reprinted, Crescent Moon 2008.

The Water is Wide. Portland: Pendragon Press 1976.

ANTHOLOGIES

Nebula Award Stories xi. Harper & Row 1977.

Edges, with Virginia Kidd. Pocket Books 1980.

Interfaces, with Virginia Kidd. Grosset & Dunlap/Ace 1980.

The Norton Book of Science Fiction, with B. Attebery, K. Fowler.
    Norton 1993.

Acknowledgments

CREDIT WHERE CREDIT IS DUE: The original idea for a birthday fest-schrift was Stan Robinson's. Debbie Notkin and Karen Joy Fowler, who know a good idea when they hear one, did solicitations and editing.

All contributions are original to this volume except for those by Molly Gloss, Ellen Kushner, Vonda N. McIntyre, and Jo Walton.

John D. Berry designed and typeset the pages and the book cover. Sandy Tilcock of Lone Goose Press designed and created the binding of the single original edition.

Carol Cooper and Nick Wood helped find contributors. Tom Whitmore supplied the signature for the front cover of the original edition. The Tiptree Award motherboard helped out with costs.

And Ursula had the birthday.